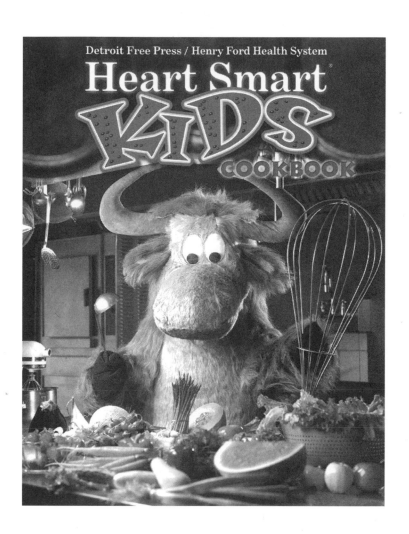

Detroit Free Press / Henry Ford Health System

Heart Smart®
KIDS
COOKBOOK

Editors and writers:
Cathy Collison and Janis Campbell

Project coordinator:
Bethany Thayer, MS, RD

Art director and designer:
Marty Westman

Photographer:
Kent Phillips

Copy Editor:
Marcy Abramson

Photo technicians:
Jessica Trevino,
Rose Ann McKean,
Christine Russell,
Kathryn Trudeau

Recipes by Henry Ford Heart Smart® registered dietitians, dietetic technicians and dietetic interns.

Recipe reader:
Sue Selasky

Thanks to Crate & Barrel of the Somerset Collection of Troy for providing us with kitchen utensils and to Schoolcraft College's culinary arts department for our cover photo location.

It is a pleasure for us at the Henry Ford Heart and Vascular Institute to share these recipes with you. We hope that you enjoy them. We have chosen ones that are favorites of our families and which will enhance your cardiovascular health.

Dr. W. Douglas Weaver

Cardiovascular disease begins at a young age. Numerous studies have shown that hardening of the arteries, or atherosclerosis, has already begun even in the teenage years. The disease is particularly common in the western world and most prevalent in those areas where dietary fat is high — such as southern Michigan. As many of you know, cardiovascular disease is the largest cause of death in the United States today, for both women and men, twice as common as the next two causes of death combined.

Beginning a healthy lifestyle and concentrating on cardiovascular health is important, and should begin with the teaching of children and promoting of cardiovascular good habits at an early age. Although cardiovascular disease is not usually manifested in men and women until they are in their 60s and 70s, the extent of the disease is greatly influenced by eating healthy, staying physically active and avoiding cigarettes in early years.

The Henry Ford Heart and Vascular Institute is dedicated to providing patients the best possible, cutting-edge, evidenced-based clinical care; training future cardiovascular specialists, and doing research that translates into new therapies and better quality of life for patients both here in Michigan as well as nationwide. The institute is recognized as one of the top 15 cardiac centers in the country and has locations throughout the Detroit metropolitan area. Our staff members are available for routine, as well as specialized cardiovascular health care.

We hope that these recipes supplement the steps you are already taking to maintain cardiovascular health. And don't forget to turn to the back of the book for more great nutritional information for parents and children. ENJOY!

W. Douglas Weaver, M.D.
Division Head, Cardiovascular Medicine
Darin Chair of Cardiology
Co-Director of Henry Ford Heart & Vascular Institute

Henry Ford Health System and the Detroit Free Press Yak's Corner would like to thank those who supported and assisted us in producing this book. A special thank you to: Norma Clark, Kelsey Collins, Jennifer Comben, Fay Fitzgerald, Steven Keteyian, Jean Lakin, Meredith Meyer, Marilyn Nack, Jeanne Stevenson, Lisa Wright and Kevin Yee

✪ **Note to kids, parents, teachers:** Be sure to read pages 128 - 144. You'll find valuable information on healthy eating — including the food pyramid — plus definitions of nutrients and a guide to fruits and vegetables that pack a punch.

CONTENTS

INTRODUCTION

Welcome to our Heart Smart®/Yak's Corner cookbook!

Good eating is like good reading — it feeds the brain and nourishes the body, and it's essential for growing up healthy.

The good news is that kids' health has generally improved in the last three decades. Kids in general are eating better and eating more good things like fruit.

The bad news? Despite efforts like the popular milk mustache campaign, kids still aren't getting enough calcium. And we're seeing double the number of overweight kids.

Kids also are skimping on servings of the vegetable and grain groups. What can you do?

Make eating together a fun family experience when you can. And when you can't eat together, pack snacks and meals that are fun and nutritious.

Having fun in the kitchen — whether you're a young cook or an experienced chef — is a great step to a lifetime of good nutrition.

Throughout this book, you'll find delicious recipes, ways to celebrate with food and nutrition advice to make sure you're eating right.

Happy cooking!

Words that really cook

Cooking's a lot easier when you know your way around the kitchen. To keep things fun and safe, you'll need an adult helper for most of these recipes. On the following pages, you will find a glossary of common cooking terms, plus a how-to guide on food preparation. (Moms and dads will find this useful, too.)

And check out the gadgets and tools on Page 8 and 9. Once you get cooking, you'll need to keep these handy.

Beat: This takes muscle power. It means to stir strongly, using a spoon, whisk or electric mixer to mix ingredients thoroughly.

Preheat: Set your oven temperature ahead of time, so the oven heats up to the required temperature.

Chop: Cut food. Some foods, like carrots, need to have the ends chopped off. You also will see this term when something needs to be cut into small chunks, but doesn't need to be neat and even.

Dice: Chop food into small even-sized chunks, smaller than 1/2 inch.

Cream: You'll see this term in lots of cookie recipes. It refers to the blending of two types of ingredients. For example, in sugar cookies you cream or mix sugar and butter or margarine. That means you mash them together until they are smooth. It's best when the butter or margarine has been softened.

Fold: We're not talking about laundry here. This term means to gently combine ingredients from the top to the bottom of your bowl. Think of folding ingredients together.

Julienne: This sounds like a girl's name, but in this case it refers to a way of cutting. If a recipe calls for julienne strips, you need to cut into very thin, and long strips.

Mince: Think teeny-tiny pieces and you've got the idea about mincing food. Mincing refers to smaller pieces than chopped.

Mix: Mixing is just that — mixing ingredients together evenly.

Sift: This is when you mix dry ingredients in a sifter so they are better distributed. You also can use a sifter for decorating, such as sifting powdered sugar over French toast.

If you're ever puzzled, most terms are common-sense ways of describing food processes.

Handy how-tos
A glossary to help you

Chopping onions:

1. On a cutting board, with a small sharp knife, cut off both ends of the onion.

2. Peel away the outer, papery layers of the onion with your hands while holding the onion under cold running water. Place the onion back on the cutting board. Throw away the peel.

3. Cut the onion in half from top to bottom.

4. Place the onion halves cut-sides down on the cutting board.

5. Holding one onion half on the board with one hand and a chef's knife in the other, cut the onion half crosswise into several slices from top to bottom.

6. Cut across the slices lengthwise about 5 or 6 times to form small, square pieces about 1/4 inch each.

7. Repeat with the other half of the onion.

Ask a grown-up to assist you the first few times you chop.

Chopping green peppers:

1. Rinse green pepper.

2. On the cutting board, use a sharp knife to cut the green pepper in half from top to bottom. Pull off the stem and throw away.

3. Remove seeds and soft white parts from inside the pepper halves and throw away.

4. Cut pepper halves into bite-size pieces.

Cutting broccoli florets:

1. Rinse broccoli.

2. Place broccoli on cutting board. With small, sharp knife, trim off floret ends off broccoli stems.

3. Save stem ends of broccoli for another use. (Or, you may purchase trimmed broccoli florets in the produce or salad-bar section of your supermarket.)

Shredding carrots:

1. With vegetable peeler, peel carrot.

2. On a cutting board, with a small, sharp knife, cut 1/4 inch off each end of carrot.

3. Coarsely grate carrot by rubbing it against large holes of grater.

Slicing celery:

1. Rinse celery and dry with paper towel.

2. Place celery on cutting board and cut into thin slices with chef's knife.

Slicing green onion:

1. Rinse green onions and place on cutting board.

2. With chef's knife cut off stringy roots and tips of green shoots.

3. With one hand, hold white part of onion on cutting board. (You may cut one, two or three onions at a time.)

4. With chef's knife, slice green and white portions into thin slices until you near the end.

Slicing radishes:

1. Rinse radishes

2. On a cutting board, with a small sharp knife, chop off ends.

3. Slice radishes into round circles.

Coring apples

1. Rinse apple.

2. On a cutting board, with a sharp knife, cut the apple in half, then in half again.

3. Using a paring knife or a melon baller, scoop the seeds and tough fibers out.

Safety smarts

Always get help from an adult for safe handling of knives and for using the oven and burners. Older yakkers, make sure you have permission before you get busy in the kitchen.

FOLLOW THESE SYMBOLS

Look for these symbols on recipes that are standout body-builders.

means this recipe supplies 60 percent or more of its calories from carbohydrates, giving you energy.

means this recipe supplies 10 grams or more of protein, a good muscle builder.

means this recipe supplies 200 mg or more of calcium, good for strong bones and healthy teeth.

means this recipe supplies at least 2 mg of iron and/or zinc, good disease fighters.

means this recipe supplies at least 1000IU of vitamin A and/or 12mg of vitamin C, which are good for healthy skin, hair and nails

Yak Fact • • • • • • • • • • • • • • • • • •

Cooks always start with clean hands. Wash up and wipe your hands dry before you start food preparation. Make sure your work surface and utensils are clean.

Everything but the kitchen sink

Here are some handy utensils you'll use over
and over again in the kitchen.

Rolling pin

Muffin pan

Colander

Grater

Steamer

Wooden spoon

Pastry
blender

Whisk

Spatula

Measuring spoons

Measuring cups

Sifter

A special thanks to Crate & Barrel, Somerset Collection, Troy.

UTENSILS

Timer

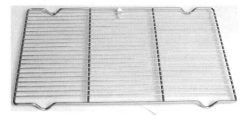

Wire cooling rack

Knife

Oven mitt/pot holder

Slotted
spoon

Peeler

Dish towels

Egg beater

Tongs

Vegetable brush

Cutting board

UTENSILS

JANUARY

Brrr! It's cold outside, but it's warm in the kitchen. January is the start of a new year and a great time to resolve to spend more time with your family. Cooking and eating are everyday celebrations of being together as a family — and all year long, you can cook up even more reasons to have celebrations each month.

January is one of Yak's favorite times — sledding, skating and playing in the snow outside. Then it's inside for something warm.

The days are short, but that's all the more reason for hanging out in the cozy kitchen. Of course, you'll kick off the new year with a celebration. It's also National Soup Month, so stir up a delicious winter soup. Our Alphabet Soup is as easy as A, B, C.

Then by the end of the month, you'll be making Super Bowl Subs for the sports fans in your family.

In between, you'll be whipping up Winter Morning Muffins… mmmm! Let's get cooking in January.

11

Photo by Kent Phillips

HEART SMART® KIDS COOKBOOK

Easy as A-B-C Alphabet Soup

INGREDIENTS:

2 medium carrots
2 medium stalks celery
1 small onion
1/2 pound chicken breast
6 cups fat-free chicken broth
1 chicken bouillon cube
1 cup uncooked alphabet macaroni
2 teaspoons chopped fresh parsley

WHAT YOU NEED:

Cutting board
Chef's knife
Measuring cups
Measuring spoons
Dutch oven or stock pot
Soup ladle

HOW YOU MAKE:

1. Slice carrots and celery (see glossary).

2. Chop onion (see glossary).

3. Cut chicken breast into bite-size pieces.

4. In a dutch oven or stock pot, heat broth, chicken bouillon cube, carrots, celery and onion to boiling, then reduce heat and simmer for approximately 20 minutes.

5. Add the alphabet macaroni (or pasta of your choice) and chicken pieces.

6. Cook until noodles are tender and chicken is cooked through, another 30 minutes.

Serve in soup bowls and garnish with parsley

Makes six 1-cup servings.

 Yak Fact · · · · · · · · · · · · · · · · · · ·
Did you know protein...
✪ builds and maintains body cells
✪ helps protect against infection
✪ builds strong bodies and provides energy!

NUTRIENT ANALYSIS PER 1-CUP SERVING:

Calories 136, fat 1g, carbohydrate 18g, protein 13g, saturated fat 0, cholesterol, 22mg, sodium 281mg, fiber 1g

FOOD EXCHANGES:
1 starch, 1 vegetable, 1 lean meat

Chocolate Oatmeal Treats

HOW YOU MAKE:

1. Spray baking dish with vegetable oil cooking spray.

2. In a large saucepan, mix together the cocoa, sugar, evaporated skim milk and oil.

3. Place over medium heat and bring to boil.

4. Allow mixture to boil one minute while stirring constantly with wooden spoon.

5. Remove from heat.

6. Quickly add peanut butter, wheat germ and rolled oats.

7. Stir until completely mixed in.

8. Pour into prepared pan and spread.

9. Allow to cool.

10. Cut into 32 pieces.

Makes 32 servings.

INGREDIENTS:

Vegetable oil cooking spray
1/4 cup unsweetened cocoa
2 cups granulated sugar
3/4 cup evaporated skim milk
2 tablespoons canola oil
1/2 cup peanut butter
1/2 cup wheat germ
3 cups rolled oats

WHAT YOU NEED:

13-inch by 9-inch baking dish
Large saucepan
Measuring cups
Measuring spoons
Wooden spoon
Knife

NUTRIENT ANALYSIS PER SERVING:

Calories 127, carbohydrate 21g, protein 3g, fat 4g, saturated fat 0.5g, cholesterol trace, fiber 1.5g, sodium 9mg

FOOD EXCHANGES:
1 1/2 starch, 1 fat

HEART SMART® KIDS COOKBOOK

Winter Morning Muffins

INGREDIENTS:

2 ripe bananas
1 cup rolled oats, uncooked
1/3 cup brown sugar, firmly packed
1/3 cup canola oil
1 teaspoon vanilla
1 cup skim milk
3 egg whites
1 1/2 cups all-purpose flour
2 teaspoons baking powder
1/8 teaspoon salt
1 teaspoon cinnamon
1/4 teaspoon allspice

WHAT YOU NEED:

Large mixing bowl
Fork
Large spoon
Large mixing bowl
Medium mixing bowl
Small mixing bowl
Measuring cups
Measuring spoons
Hand mixer or wire whisk
Rubber spatula
Muffin tin
16 paper baking cups
Wire cooling rack
Oven mitts

HOW YOU MAKE:

1. Preheat oven to 400 degrees Fahrenheit.

2. Peel bananas. Using a fork, mash bananas in a medium size bowl.

3. In a large mixing bowl, using a large spoon, combine oats, brown sugar, oil, vanilla, mashed bananas and milk. Mix well and set aside.

4. Put egg whites into a small bowl. Using a hand mixer or wire whisk, whip until fluffy, cleaning sides of bowl with rubber spatula.

5. Fold egg whites into the oat mixture.

6. In a medium bowl, combine flour, baking powder, salt, cinnamon and allspice.

7. Gradually add flour mixture to batter. Mix after each addition.

8. Line muffin pans with 16 paper baking cups. Using a spoon, pour batter into cups, filling each about two-thirds full.

9. Bake 18 to 20 minutes or until golden brown. Using oven mitts, remove from oven and cool on wire cooling racks.

Makes 16 muffins.

NUTRIENT ANALYSIS PER MUFFIN:

Calories 147, carbohydrate 22g, protein 3g, fat 5g, saturated fat 0.5g, cholesterol trace, fiber 1.5g, sodium 84mg

FOOD EXCHANGES:
1 1/2 starch, 1 fat

Super Bowl Subs

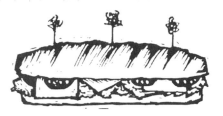

HOW YOU MAKE:

1. Wash and slice tomatoes, onion and green pepper (see glossary).

2. Using a long serrated knife, on a large cutting board cut the loaf of bread horizontally in half.

3. Using a small spatula, spread the bottom half with mustard.

4. Layer the mozzarella cheese, turkey and ham on top of the mustard.

5. Top with shredded lettuce, sliced tomato, onion and green pepper.

6. Drizzle the Italian salad dressing over the vegetables.

7. Top with the remaining bread half.

8. On a cutting board, using a long serrated knife, cut into 8 even servings.

Makes 8 servings.

INGREDIENTS:

2 medium tomatoes
1 medium onion
1 medium green pepper
1 loaf (16 ounces) unsliced French bread
2 tablespoons prepared mustard
4 ounces mozzarella cheese made with part-skim milk, thinly sliced
2 cups shredded lettuce
4 ounces sliced turkey breast
2 ounces sliced lean ham
1/4 cup low-fat Italian dressing

WHAT YOU NEED:
Cutting board
Chef's knife
Long serrated knife
Small spatula
Measuring spoons
Measuring cups

NUTRIENT ANALYSIS PER SERVING:

Calories 244, carbohydrate 34g, protein 15g, fat 5g, saturated fat 2g, cholesterol 22mg, fiber 2.5g, sodium 618mg

FOOD EXCHANGES:
2 starch, 1 vegetable, 1 meat

Cheesy Vegetable Stuffed Potato

INGREDIENTS:

4 large baking potatoes
10-ounce package frozen
California blend vegetables,
thawed
1 cup low-fat processed
cheese sauce

WHAT YOU NEED:

Vegetable brush
Fork
Wooden spoon
Large sharp knife
Measuring cup
Oven mitt

HOW YOU MAKE:

1. Wash and scrub potatoes with vegetable brush. Prick the skin of the potato with a fork. Microwave potatoes on high about 10 minutes until fork-tender.

2. Using oven mitt, remove potatoes from microwave oven. Cut each potato in half. Top potato with vegetables and cheese sauce.

3. Return to microwave oven for about 2 minutes until cheese melts.

Makes 4 servings.

NUTRIENT ANALYSIS PER SERVING:

Calories 302, carbohydrate 58g, protein 11g, fat 3g, saturated fat 2g, cholesterol 10mg, fiber 7g, sodium 547mg

FOOD EXCHANGES:
3 starch, 2 vegetable, 1/2 fat

Yakaroni and Cheese

HOW YOU MAKE:

1. Preheat oven to 350 degrees Fahrenheit.

2. In a large saucepan, cook macaroni according to package directions, omitting the salt and leaving the macaroni slightly undercooked; drain the macaroni.

3. In a blender or food processor, process the cottage cheese until smooth, scraping sides of blender with rubber spatula.

4. In a medium mixing bowl, using a wire whisk, slightly beat the egg whites. Then mix in the skim milk. Using rubber spatula, add cottage cheese, cheddar cheese, salt, white pepper and parsley. Blend well.

5. Add cooked macaroni and mix.

6. Spray 1-quart baking dish with vegetable oil cooking spray. Pour macaroni mixture into baking dish.

7. In a small bowl, with mixing spoon, combine bread crumbs, parmesan cheese and paprika. Sprinkle on top of macaroni mixture.

8. Bake in oven for 1 hour.

9. Remove from oven using oven mitts. Put on heat resistant surface.

Makes 8 servings.

INGREDIENTS:

2 cups uncooked macaroni
3 cups fat free cottage cheese
2 egg whites
1 cup skim milk
1 cup (4 ounces) shredded extra-sharp cheddar cheese
1/8 teaspoon salt
1/2 teaspoon white pepper
1 tablespoon chopped fresh parsley
Vegetable oil cooking spray
2 tablespoons bread crumbs
2 teaspoons fat-free grated Parmesan cheese
1/2 teaspoon paprika

WHAT YOU NEED:

Large saucepan
Wooden spoon, mixing spoon
Colander
Blender or food processor
Rubber spatula
Medium mixing bowl
Wire whisk
Measuring cups, spoons
1 quart baking dish
Small mixing bowl

NUTRIENT ANALYSIS PER SERVING:

Calories 239, carbohydrate 26g, protein 20g, fat 5g, saturated fat 3g, cholesterol 15mg, fiber 1g, sodium 465mg

FOOD EXCHANGES:
2 starch, 2 lean meat

FEBRUARY

There are so many reasons to celebrate February. Just when you need a boost in the middle of winter, along comes Valentine's Day. The Yak loves exchanging valentines, planning a family party and taking time to tell his best buddies how much he likes them.

But that isn't all there is to love about cooking in February. Put a little cherry in your Presidents' Day (make a Pineapple-Cherry Cake).

The month is sweet. And it's healthy, too. Not surprisingly, February is American Heart Month. And we've got recipes so tasty no one will know how Heart Smart® they really are.

Photo by Kent Phillips

Chocolate Brownie Hearts

INGREDIENTS:

Vegetable oil cooking spray
3 tablespoons canola oil
3/4 cup granulated sugar
2 egg whites
1/4 cup unsweetened cocoa
3/4 cup sifted flour
1 teaspoon baking powder
1/2 teaspoon vanilla extract
Powdered sugar

WHAT YOU NEED:

8-inch by 8-inch by 2-inch
baking pan
2 medium mixing bowls
Spoon
1 small bowl
Wire whisk or hand mixer
Rubber spatula
Measuring cups
Measuring spoons
Sifter
Wire cooling rack
Heart-shaped cookie cutter

HOW YOU MAKE:

1. Preheat oven to 350 degrees Fahrenheit.

2. Spray an 8-inch by 8-inch by 2-inch baking pan with vegetable oil cooking spray. Set aside.

3. In a medium bowl, with a spoon, blend together the oil and sugar.

4. In a small bowl, using a wire whisk or hand mixer, beat egg whites. Add to the oil and sugar mixture, cleaning sides of bowl with rubber spatula.

5. In a medium bowl, using a sifter, sift together the cocoa, flour and baking powder.

6. Add the flour mixture to the liquid mixture and thoroughly combine. Add vanilla extract. Mix.

7. Pour the batter into the prepared pan and bake for 25 minutes.

8. Using oven mitts, remove from the oven and cool slightly on wire cooling rack. Cut into hearts with heart-shaped cookie cutter. Sprinkle with powdered sugar.

Makes 9 - 12 hearts.

NUTRIENT ANALYSIS PER SERVING:

Calories 152, carbohydrate 25g, protein 2g, fat 5g, saturated fat 0.5g, fiber 0.5g, sodium 59mg

FOOD EXCHANGES:
1 1/2 starch, 1 fat

Cupid's Crush Muffins

HOW YOU MAKE:

1. Place peppermint candies in a heavy-duty zippered-top plastic bag. Using a rolling pin, crush the candy.

2. Preheat oven to 400 degrees Fahrenheit.

3. Line medium muffin cups with paper baking cups.

4. In a large bowl, using a hand mixer or wire whisk, beat milk, applesauce, vanilla and egg whites, cleaning sides of bowl with rubber spatula.

5. Dump in flour, sugar, cocoa, baking powder and salt. Stir until flour is moistened (batter will be lumpy).

6. Using large spoon, fold in chocolate chips and crushed peppermint candy.

7. Using 1/4-cup measuring cup, divide batter evenly among 12 muffin cups.

8. Bake 20 to 25 minutes or until golden brown.

9. Using oven mitts, remove muffins immediately and allow to cool on a wire rack.

Makes 12 muffins.

INGREDIENTS:

18 round peppermint candies
1 cup skim milk
1/4 cup applesauce
1/2 teaspoon vanilla
2 egg whites
2 cups flour
1/3 cup sugar
1/3 cup unsweetened cocoa powder
1 tablespoon baking powder
1/2 teaspoon salt
1/2 cup reduced-fat chocolate chips

WHAT YOU NEED:

Heavy duty zippered-top plastic bag
Rolling pin
Muffin pan
12 paper baking cups
Hand mixer or wire whisk
Large bowl
Rubber spatula
Medium bowl
Measuring cups
Measuring spoons
Wire rack

NUTRIENT ANALYSIS PER MUFFIN:

Calories 198, carbohydrate 40g, protein 4g, fat 3g, saturated fat 2.5g, cholesterol trace, fiber 1g, sodium 214mg

FOOD EXCHANGES:
2 1/2 starch, 1 fat

Hearty Meat Loaf

INGREDIENTS:

Vegetable oil cooking spray
1 large onion
1 medium green bell pepper
1 large celery rib
2 carrots
1 teaspoon thyme
1 pound very lean ground beef
1 pound ground turkey breast
1/4 cup old-fashioned oats
1/4 cup wheat germ
2/3 cup chili sauce, divided
1/4 cup skim milk
4 egg whites
1 teaspoon salt
1 1/2 teaspoons freshly ground pepper

WHAT YOU NEED:

Cutting board
Sharp knife
Grater
Large skillet
Wooden spoon
Large bowl
Measuring cups
Measuring spoons
8 1/2-inch by 4-inch baking pan
Large spoon
Meat thermometer
Oven mitts
Oven rack
Metal spatula

HOW YOU MAKE:

1. On a cutting board, with a sharp knife, chop onion, green pepper and celery.

2. Using a grater, grate carrots.

3. Spray a large skillet with the vegetable oil cooking spray. Add the onion, green pepper, celery, carrots and thyme. Cook over low heat, stirring once or twice until the vegetables are very soft.

4. Remove from heat; set on a burner not in use to cool to room temperature.

5. Preheat the oven to 350 degrees Fahrenheit.

Yak Fact • • • • • • • •

Did you know iron...
✪ helps the body use energy
✪ carries oxygen to the cells
and helps prevent infection!

6. In a large bowl, combine the cooked vegetables, the ground beef and the ground turkey.

7. Add the oats, wheat germ, 1/3 cup of the chili sauce, skim milk, egg whites, salt and pepper. Mix well.

8. Spoon the meat mixture into an 8 1/2-inch by 4-inch baking dish.

9. Smooth the top with the back of a spoon.

10. Spread the remaining 1/3 cup of chili sauce over the loaf. Bake meat loaf for 1 hour, or until it is just cooked through and shows no trace of pink (a meat thermometer will register 165 degrees in the center of the loaf).

11. Remove from the oven, using oven mitts, and place on an oven rack and let meat loaf stand for about 10 minutes. Then slice and serve with a metal spatula.

Makes 8 servings.

PHOTO BY KENT PHILLIPS

NUTRIENT ANALYSIS PER SERVING:

Calories 251, carbohydrate 14g, protein 25g, fat 10g, saturated fat 3.5g, cholesterol 71mg, fiber 2g, sodium 623mg

FOOD EXCHANGES:
1 starch, 3 lean meat

Hot Tuna Pockets

INGREDIENTS:

1 stalk celery
2 green onions
One 8-ounce block of fat-free cream cheese
1/4 cup snipped fresh parsley
Black pepper to taste
2 cans (about 6 ounces each) tuna, packed in water, drained
1 loaf (1 pound) frozen bread dough, thawed
8 teaspoons all-purpose flour, divided
1 egg white

WHAT YOU NEED:

Cutting board
Sharp knife
Small bowl
Measuring cups
Measuring spoons
Kitchen shears
Large spoon
Fork
Pancake turner
Wire whisk
Rolling pin
Cookie sheet
Pastry brush

HOW YOU MAKE:

1. Chop celery (see glossary).

2. Slice green onions (see glossary).

3. In a small bowl, soften cream cheese with a spoon. Add celery, green onion, parsley and black pepper. Mix until smooth.

4. Fold in the tuna. Set aside.

5. Divide the bread dough into 8 equal-sized pieces. Shape each into a ball and flatten into a small disc.

6. Make a lightly floured surface, using 1 teaspoon of flour for each piece of dough. Using a rolling pin, on the floured surface, roll each piece into a circle about 5 to 6 inches in diameter.

7. Spoon about 1/4 cup of the tuna mixture over half of each circle.

8. Fold the dough over the filling to make a half circle and firmly pinch the edges together to seal. You also can seal edges by pressing with the tines of a lightly floured fork.

9. Transfer to cookie sheet using a pancake turner.

10. In a small bowl, slightly beat egg white with a wire whisk.

11. Using a pastry brush, brush the top of each pocket with egg white. Bake until golden and puffed, about 20 minutes.

12. Using oven mitts, remove from oven and serve.

Cook's Note: Choose tuna that has no more than 3 grams of fat per 2-ounce serving.

Makes 8 pockets.

NUTRIENT ANALYSIS PER POCKET:

Calories 261, carbohydrate 42g, protein 16g, fat 3.5g, saturated fat 0.5g, cholesterol 9mg, fiber 1g, sodium 614mg

FOOD EXCHANGES:
2 1/2 starch, 1 1/2 lean meat

Oven-Fried Fish Sticks

INGREDIENTS:

1 pound cod
1/4 cup cornmeal
1/4 cup seasoned dry bread crumbs
1/2 cup skim milk
Vegetable oil cooking spray
1/3 cup low-fat mayonnaise
1 teaspoon lemon juice
2 tablespoons sweet pickle relish

WHAT YOU NEED:

13-inch by 9-inch by 2-inch baking pan
Measuring cups
Measuring spoons
Sharp knife
Small dish
Small bowl
Oven mitts

HOW YOU MAKE:

1. Move oven rack to position slightly above middle of oven.

2. Heat oven to 500 degrees Fahrenheit.

3. Cut cod into 3-inch by 1-inch pieces.

4. Mix cornmeal and bread crumbs together in small dish.

5. Dip fish into milk, then coat with cornmeal-bread crumb mixture.

6. Place fish in ungreased baking pan.

7. Spray vegetable oil cooking spray over fish.

8. Bake uncovered about 10 minutes or until fish flakes easily with a fork.

9. In a small bowl, mix mayonnaise, lemon juice and pickle relish. Refrigerate until ready to serve with fish.

Makes 4 servings.

NUTRIENT ANALYSIS PER SERVING:

Calories 218, carbohydrate 20g, protein 22g, fat 5g, saturated fat 1g, cholesterol 52mg, fiber 1g, sodium 448 mg.

FOOD EXCHANGES:
1 starch, 2 1/2 lean meats

Pineapple-Cherry Cake

HOW YOU MAKE:

1. Preheat oven to 350 degrees Fahrenheit.

2. Spray a 9-inch by 13-inch baking pan with the vegetable oil cooking spray.

3. Dump in the cherry pie filling and spread to fill pan.

4. Dump in the pineapple and juice and swirl until cherry pie filling and pineapple are evenly distributed.

5. Sprinkle the cake mix over the top.

6. Drizzle the melted margarine on top.

7. Place in oven and bake for about one hour.

8. Using oven mitts, remove cake from oven and allow to cool before serving.

Makes 16 servings.

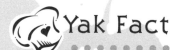

Yak Fact

Many margarines contain trans-fatty acids that are bad for your heart. When buying margarines look for ones that say they contain "no-trans fats."

INGREDIENTS:

Vegetable oil cooking spray
1 can (20 ounces) cherry pie filling
1 can (20 ounces) crushed pineapple in light syrup
1 box (18.25-ounces) low-fat yellow cake mix
1/2 cup margarine with no-trans fats (melted)

WHAT YOU NEED:

9-inch by 13-inch baking pan
Measuring cups
Spatula
Oven mitts

NUTRIENT ANALYSIS PER SERVING:

Calories 232, carbohydrate 43g, protein 2g, fat 6.5g, saturated fat 1.5g, cholesterol 0mg, fiber 0.5g, sodium 284mg

FOOD EXCHANGES:
2 fruits, 1 starch, 1 1/2 fat

MARCH

Go Green! St. Patrick's Day doesn't just belong to the Irish anymore. You'll have fun whipping up a green-themed family dinner. (Start with a green veggie dip that's good for you.) Plus, you can march into the month with some other themes: It's National Peanut Month and National Noodle Month.

Of course, celebrations can be any time of day. It's maple syrup time in March, a great time to have our Fabulous French Toast. And did you know that Johnny Appleseed Day is March 11? It's a day to salute legendary apple-tree grower Johnny Chapman with our Awesome Apple Cake.

March is also National Nutrition Month. So make the most of March in the kitchen.

Photo by Kent Phillips

Very Green Veggie Dip

MARCH

INGREDIENTS:

1 cup fat-free sour cream
2 tablespoons dried onion soup mix
3-4 drops green food coloring
1/2 medium cucumber
1 small green pepper
1 medium stalk celery
2 ounces broccoli (should be about 1/2 cup of florets)

WHAT YOU NEED:

Cutting board
Chef's knife
Small bowl with cover
Measuring cups
Measuring spoons

HOW YOU MAKE:

1. In a small bowl, mix the sour cream, dried onion soup mix and green food coloring.

2. Cover and place in the refrigerator for 3 to 4 hours.

3. Slice cucumbers and green pepper into strips, celery into sticks and broccoli into florets (see glossary).

4. When ready, remove dip from the refrigerator and serve with cucumbers, green pepper sticks, celery sticks and broccoli florets.

Cook's Note: Instead of serving the dip in a bowl, hollow out a small loaf of round bread or a large green pepper and place the dip in that.

Tip: Think of other green vegetables: asparagus, pea pods, etc.

Makes 4 servings.

 Yak Fact •

Did you know Vitamin C ...
✪ hastens healing of wounds and bones.

NUTRIENT ANALYSIS PER SERVING:

Calories 67, carbohydrate 14g, protein 3g, fat 0, saturated fat 0, cholesterol 6mg, fiber 1g, sodium 325mg

FOOD EXCHANGES:
1 vegetable, 1/2 starch

Fabulous French Toast

HOW TO MAKE:

1. In a small bowl, mash banana with a fork.

2. In a medium mixing bowl slightly beat the egg and egg whites together with a wire whisk.

3. To the egg mixture, add honey, cinnamon, milk and mashed banana and mix well.

4. Pour mixture into a shallow dish such as a baking pan.

5. Spray vegetable oil cooking spray onto the griddle or skillet.

6. Heat griddle or skillet to medium heat.

7. Using a fork, dip bread into the egg mixture, turning to coat both sides.

8. Place each slice on griddle and cook about 4 minutes on each side, flipping with a pancake turner or until golden brown.

Makes 10 slices.

Cook's Note: Children under the age of 1 should not eat honey.

INGREDIENTS:

1 over-ripe banana
1 whole egg
2 egg whites
1 tablespoon honey
1/4 cup skim milk
1/4 teaspoon cinnamon
Vegetable oil cooking spray
10 slices whole wheat bread

WHAT YOU NEED:

Small mixing bowl
Fork
Medium mixing bowl
Wire whisk
Measuring cups
Measuring spoons
8-inch baking pan
Griddle or skillet
Pancake turner

NUTRIENT INFORMATION PER SLICE:

Calories 101, carbohydrate 18g, protein 4g, fat 2g, saturated fat 0.5g, cholesterol 20mg, fiber 2.5g, sodium 185mg

FOOD EXCHANGES:
1 starch, 1/2 fat

Awesome Apple Cake

INGREDIENTS:

6-7 medium tart apples
Vegetable oil cooking spray
3 tablespoons tub margarine
3/4 cup sugar
2 egg whites
1 teaspoon vanilla
1 cup sifted flour
1 teaspoon baking soda
1/2 teaspoon cinnamon
1/2 teaspoon nutmeg
1/4 cup chopped nuts
1/4 cup raisins
1/4 cup wheat germ

WHAT YOU NEED:

Sharp knife
Cutting board
8-inch square baking pan
Large mixing bowl
Rubber spatula
Medium mixing bowl
Measuring spoons
Measuring cups

HOW YOU MAKE:

1. Preheat oven to 350 degrees Fahrenheit.

2. Peel and dice the apples (see glossary).

3. Spray an 8-inch square baking pan with vegetable oil cooking spray.

4. In a large mixing bowl, using a rubber spatula, cream margarine and sugar together.

5. Add egg whites and vanilla to the margarine and sugar and mix well.

6. In a medium mixing bowl, sift together flour, baking soda and spices.

7. Add flour mixture to creamed mixture and mix well.

8. Stir in diced apples, nuts, raisins and wheat germ.

9. Pour mixture into 8-inch baking pan.

10. Place pan in oven for 40-45 minutes.

11. Using oven mitts, remove from oven and place on wire cooling rack.

Makes 9 servings.

NUTRIENT ANALYSIS PER SERVING:

Calories 245, carbohydrate 45g, protein 4g, fat 6g, saturated fat 1g, cholesterol 0mg, fiber 3g, sodium 204mg.

FOOD EXCHANGES:
2 starch, 1 fruit, 1 fat

Dinner Pie

HOW YOU MAKE:

1. Chop onion and green pepper (see glossary).

2. Preheat oven to 400 degrees Fahrenheit.

3. Spray a medium size skillet with vegetable oil cooking spray. Add chopped onion and green pepper and cook until onion is soft, stirring with wooden spoon.

4. Add ground turkey. Cook, breaking up the meat and stirring occasionally until brown. Stir in 1/2 packet of chili or taco seasonings and tomato sauce. Return to simmer for approximately 10 minutes.

5. Separate crescent dough into 8 triangles. Place in ungreased 8- or 9-inch pie plate. Press over the bottom and up sides to form crust.

6. Sprinkle 1/4 cup Parmesan cheese over crust bottom. Spoon 1/2 of the turkey mixture into crust; sprinkle shredded cheese over mixture.

7. Spoon remaining meat mixture over cheese and top with remaining Parmesan cheese.

8. Bake 15-20 minutes until crust is golden brown. Remove from oven with oven mitts and set on cooling rack. Cut the sliced mozzarella cheese into lengthwise strips and arrange on pie in criss-cross pattern.

9. Allow pie to sit approximately 10 minutes before serving so the topping melts.

Makes 6 servings.

INGREDIENTS:

1 medium onion
1 small green bell pepper
Vegetable oil cooking spray
1 pound ground turkey breast
1/2 packet taco or chili seasoning mix
1 can (15 ounce) no-added salt tomato sauce
1 can (8 ounce) reduced-fat crescent dinner rolls
1/2 cup fat-free Parmesan cheese, divided
1/2 cup shredded fat-free mozzarella cheese
2 ounces sliced part-skim mozzarella cheese

WHAT YOU NEED:

Cutting board
Sharp knife
Medium size skillet
Wooden spoon
8- or 9-inch pie plate
Large spoon
Measuring cups
Oven mitts
Cooling rack

NUTRIENT ANALYSIS PER SERVING:

Calories 315, carbohydrate 25g, protein 30g, fat 10g, saturated fat 2.5g, cholesterol 60mg, fiber 2g, sodium 850mg

FOOD EXCHANGES:
2 starch, 3 1/2 meat

Spicy Potato Skins

MARCH

INGREDIENTS:

6 large baking potatoes
1 tomato
2 medium green onions
Vegetable oil cooking spray
1 teaspoon chili powder
2 tablespoons imitation
bacon bits
1 cup (4 ounces) shredded,
lowfat cheddar cheese
1/2 cup fat-free sour cream

WHAT YOU NEED:

Vegetable brush
Cutting board
Sharp knife
Fork
Oven mitts
Microwave-safe plate
Baking sheet
Measuring cups
Measuring spoons
Spoon

HOW YOU MAKE:

1. Scrub baking potatoes with vegetable brush.

2. Finely chop tomatoes and chop green onions (see glossary).

3. Prick potatoes all over with a fork. Arrange on a microwave-safe plate. Microwave, uncovered, on 100 percent power (high) for 17 to 22 minutes or until almost tender, rearranging once. Or, bake potatoes in a preheated 425 degree Fahrenheit oven for 40 to 45 minutes or until tender. Using oven mitts, remove and cool.

4. On a cutting board, with a sharp knife, cut potatoes lengthwise into quarters.

5. Scoop out the inside of each potato section, leaving about 1 1/4-inch thick shell. (Cover and chill the potato insides for another use.)

NUTRIENT ANALYSIS PER PIECE:

Calories 52, carbohydrate 8g, protein 2g, fat 1g, saturated fat 0.5g, cholesterol 4mg, fiber 1.5g, sodium 63mg

FOOD EXCHANGES:
1/2 starch

6. Preheat oven to 450 degrees.

7. Place potato skins on a baking sheet. Spray insides with vegetable oil cooking spray.

8. Sprinkle with chili powder, bacon bits and tomato.

9. Top with low-fat cheese.

10. Bake for 10 to 12 minutes or until cheese melts and potato sections are heated through.

11. Using oven mitts, remove from oven.

12. Serve with sour cream and green onions.

Makes 24 pieces.

Yak Fact ● ● ● ● ● ● ● ● ●

Did you know...

✪ A carbohydrate provides energy and is the major energy source for the central nervous system. Carbohydrates help the body use fat and provide fiber, too.

✪ Not all fat is bad. Fat provides energy and forms part of every cell. Fat carries vitamins A, D, E and K, known as fat-soluble vitamins.

The Best Bagel

INGREDIENTS:

1 bagel
1 tablespoon natural
peanut butter
1/2 tablespoon grape jelly
1 tablespoon wheat germ
1/2 tablespoon raisins

WHAT YOU NEED:

Long serrated knife
Cutting board
Measuring spoons
Table knife

HOW YOU MAKE:

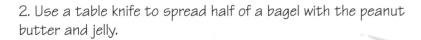

1. Using a long serrated knife, on a cutting board slice the bagel horizontally in half.

2. Use a table knife to spread half of a bagel with the peanut butter and jelly.

3. Sprinkle wheat germ over the jelly.

4. Sprinkle with the raisins.

5. Put the second half of bagel on top. (Can store overnight.)

Makes 1 serving.

COOK'S NOTE: Some bagels can be bought pre-sliced.

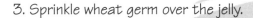

NUTRIENT ANALYSIS PER SERVING:

Calories 358, carbohydrate 55g, protein 13g, fat 10g, saturated fat 1g, cholesterol 0mg, fiber 4g, sodium 443mg

FOOD EXCHANGES:
3 starch, 1/2 fruit, 1/2 meat, 1 1/2 fat

Noodle Kugel

HOW YOU MAKE:

1. Preheat oven to 350 degrees Fahrenheit.

2. Spray an 8-inch by 8-inch or 1 1/2-quart casserole dish with vegetable oil cooking spray; set aside.

3. Cook noodles according to package directions, omitting salt.

4. Drain and rinse under cold water.

5. In a small bowl, beat egg whites with a fork until foamy.

6. In a medium-size mixing bowl, combine the cottage cheese, yogurt, pineapple, beaten egg whites and melted margarine.

7. Add cooked and drained noodles and mix until noodles are covered with mixture.

8. Place the noodle mixture in prepared pan. Bake for an hour.

9. Sprinkle the kugel with brown sugar. Increase the oven temperature to 400 degrees Fahrenheit and bake an additional 15 minutes or until the noodles are browned on top.

10. Remove from oven using oven mitts, and let it sit on a wire cooling rack until cool. Cut and serve with a metal spatula.

Makes 6 servings.

INGREDIENTS:

Vegetable oil cooking spray
2 1/2 cups (4 ounces) medium-cut, no-yolk noodles
1/2 cup lowfat cottage cheese
1 cup nonfat plain yogurt
1/2 cup crushed pineapple, with juice
2 egg whites
1 tablespoon melted, unsalted, no trans-fats margarine
2 tablespoons brown sugar

WHAT YOU NEED:

8-inch by 8-inch casserole dish
Large pot
Wooden spoon
Colander
Small bowl
Fork
Medium mixing bowl
Large mixing spoon
Measuring cups
Measuring spoons
Oven mitts
Wire cooling rack
Metal spatula

NUTRIENT ANALYSIS PER SERVING:

Calories 156, carbohydrate 23g, protein 9g, fat 3g, saturated fat 1g, cholesterol 27mg, fiber 0.5g, sodium 155mg

FOOD EXCHANGES:
1 starch, 1/2 fruit, 1 meat

APRIL

April showers bring... rainy days. How about making a Rainy Day Dirt Cake to dig into? The Yak loves putting on rubber boots and jumping in puddles. But why not get a little messy inside, too?

You can fool around in the kitchen for April Fools' Day with our Magical Muffins recipe.

Many families celebrate Easter by boiling and dyeing eggs. What do you do with all those eggs after you've colored them? The Yak has an eggs-cellent idea. Make some Radish Rabbits.

No fooling, this month is filled with fun.

Photo by Kent Phillips

Magical Muffins

APRIL

INGREDIENTS:

1 1/2 cups all-purpose flour
1/4 cup white sugar
2 teaspoons baking powder
1/2 teaspoon baking soda
3 tablespoons canola oil
1 cup non-fat plain yogurt
1/4 cup skim milk
2 egg whites
1/2 teaspoon vanilla
Vegetable oil cooking spray
2 tablespoons raspberry
jam or jelly, divided (or
other flavor)

WHAT YOU NEED:

Large mixing bowl
Medium mixing bowl
Measuring cups
Measuring spoons
Mixing spoon
Muffin tin (for 12 muffins)

HOW YOU MAKE:

1. Preheat oven to 375 degrees Fahrenheit.

2. In a large mixing bowl, mix flour, sugar, baking powder and baking soda.

3. In a small mixing bowl mix oil, yogurt and milk.

4. Beat in to liquid mixture, egg whites and vanilla.

5. Slowly add liquid mixture to dry mixture, stirring until moistened.

6. Spray muffin tin with vegetable oil cooking spray.

7. Using a small measuring cup, spoon half the batter into 12 muffin cups.

8. Place about 1/2 teaspoon raspberry jam or jelly on top of batter in each of the 12 muffin cups.

9. Spoon rest of batter on top of the raspberry jam or jelly.

10. Place muffin tin in oven and bake for 15-20 minutes or until golden brown. Using oven mitts, immediately remove muffins from oven and transfer to a wire rack. Serve warm or cool.

Makes 12 muffins.

NUTRIENT ANALYSIS PER MUFFIN:

Calories 127, carbohydrate 20g, protein 4g, fat 4g, saturated fat 0.5g, cholesterol trace, fiber 0.5g, sodium 142mg

FOOD EXCHANGES:
1 starch, 1/2 fat

Tasty Tuna Salad

HOW YOU MAKE:

1. On a cutting board, using a paring knife, cut each egg in half and remove and discard the egg yolk.

2. Use the knife to coarsely chop the egg whites.

3. Next, use the knife to cut the green grapes in half and to chop the red onion (see glossary).

4. In a medium bowl, combine the tuna, egg whites, grapes, red onion, lemon zest and pepper. Toss gently with a fork.

5. In a small bowl, mix mayonnaise and sour cream together with a spoon. Toss with the tuna salad.

6. Serve on a leaf of lettuce.

Makes 4 servings.

INGREDIENTS:

2 cans (about 6 ounces) water-packed tuna, well-drained
6 hard-boiled eggs
1/2 cup seedless green grapes
1 medium red onion
1-2 teaspoons finely grated lemon zest, or rind, to taste
Freshly ground black pepper, to taste
1/2 cup low-fat mayonnaise
1/4 cup fat-free sour cream
4 lettuce leaves

WHAT YOU NEED:

Cutting board
Small paring or chef's knife
Medium mixing bowl
Small mixing bowl
Fork
Rubber spatula

NUTRIENT ANALYSIS PER SERVING:

Calories 262, carbohydrate 13g, protein 28g, fat 11g, saturated fat 2g, cholesterol 37mg, fiber 1g, sodium 574mg

FOOD EXCHANGES:
1/2 starch, 1/2 fruit, 4 lean meat

APRIL

Rainy Day Dirt Cake

INGREDIENTS:

20-ounce package of reduced-fat chocolate sandwich cookies
4 cups skim milk
2 (3.4 ounce) packages instant chocolate pudding
12 ounces frozen fat-free whipped topping, partially thawed
2 (8 ounce) fat-free cream cheese blocks
4-5 gummy worms

WHAT YOU NEED:

Large resealable plastic bag
Rolling pin
Small bowl
Medium mixing bowl
Hand mixer
Rubber spatula
1 seven-inch unused plastic flower pot or sand bucket, clean
Plastic wrap
Silk, plastic or real flowers for garnish
Garden trowel, clean, for serving, optional

HOW YOU MAKE:

1. Place cookies in a large resealable bag. Seal the bag, being careful to get most of the air out, and place on hard surface. Take a rolling pin and roll over the bag enough times to crush to cookies.

2. In small bowl, soften cream cheese with a rubber spatula.

3. In a medium bowl, mix the milk and pudding together with a mixer on the lowest setting.

4. Next, mix in the whipped topping. Then mix in the cream cheese. Mix well.

5. Cover the bottom of a plastic flower pot with a plastic lid, piece of foil or a piece of plastic wrap to block the drainage hole.

6. Sprinkle in a layer of cookie crumbs. Top with a layer of the pudding mixture.

7. Repeat, making several layers of each, ending with cookie crumbs on top.

8. Cover with plastic wrap and refrigerate overnight.

9. Before serving, "plant" the flowers and place the gummy worms on the "dirt," if desired.

10. To serve, use a clean garden trowel or spoon.

Makes twenty 1/2-cup servings.

NUTRIENT ANALYSIS PER SERVING:

Calories 258, carbohydrate 47g, protein 8g, fat 5g, saturated fat 1g, cholesterol 3mg, fiber 1g, sodium 474mg

FOOD EXCHANGES:
3 starch, 1 fat

Radish Rabbits

HOW YOU MAKE:

1. Peel the shell from hard-boiled egg. Then set egg aside.

2. Slice vegetables for your bunny's face (with adult help). Cut radishes in half lengthwise (you'll want longer side for bunny ears), then cut again for a 1/4 inch slice. Choose the longest slices for bunny ears. Using the knife, cut a rabbit-ear shape. (See photo on page 39.)

3. Cut a thin slice atop each side of egg, then insert radish ears. Cut additional radish triangle shapes for nose and mouth if desired.

4. Push two peppercorns in egg for eyes.

5. Cut slot for julienned carrots and place as short strands for whiskers.

Makes 4 rabbits.

INGREDIENTS:

4 hard-boiled eggs
8 peppercorns
4 radishes
Julienned carrots (see glossary)

WHAT YOU NEED:

Sharp knife
Cutting board
Pretty plate for display

Yak Fact

Eggs are a great source of high-quality protein with good amounts of vitamins A, D and B12. The yolk of the egg is high in cholesterol. While healthy kids and adults can handle the cholesterol, some people's blood cholesterol levels rise with high cholesterol foods, putting them at risk for heart disease. We recommend limiting egg yolks to 2 to 3 per week.

NUTRIENT ANALYSIS PER EGG:

Calories 80, carbohydrate 1g, protein 6g, fat 5g, saturated fat 1.5g, cholesterol 212 mg, fiber 0, sodium 164 mg

FOOD EXCHANGES:
1 medium-fat meat

Vegetable Deviled Eggs

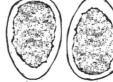

INGREDIENTS

1/4 of a small onion
1 medium raw carrot
1 medium celery stalk
1 cup fat-free cottage
cheese, drained
2 tablespoons low-fat
mayonnaise or salad
dressing
1/2 teaspoon sugar
15 hard-boiled eggs
Parsley (optional for
garnish)

WHAT YOU NEED:

Cutting board
Sharp knife
Food processor
Small spoon
Measuring cups
Measuring spoons

HOW YOU MAKE:

1. Dice onion (see glossary).

2. Peel and cut carrot in 1-inch pieces.

3. Place onion, carrot and celery in food processor with metal blade inserted and chop fine.

4. Add cottage cheese, mayonnaise, sugar and lemon juice to mix and blend in processor until smooth.

5. Peel the hard-boiled eggs and cut in half lengthwise. Scoop out yellow yolk and throw away.

6. Place approximately 1 tablespoon of mixture into each egg white half. Garnish with parsley if desired.

Makes 15 servings of 2 halves each.

 Yak Fact ···············

Food gives you energy — for playing, working, thinking, learning and just hanging around!

NUTRIENT ANALYSIS PER 2 HALVES:

Calories 34, carbohydrate 2g, protein 5g, fat 0, saturated fat 0, cholesterol 0mg, fiber trace, sodium 128mg

FOOD EXCHANGES:
1/2 lean meat, 1/2 vegetable

Banana Breakfast Shake

HOW YOU MAKE:

1. Peel and freeze one ripe banana. On a cutting board, using a sharp knife, slice banana.

2. Place the frozen banana slices, skim milk, cottage cheese, honey, vanilla extract and chocolate syrup in a blender.

3. Process mixture until smooth and creamy. Clean sides of blender with rubber spatula.

4. Serve in a tall glass.

Cook's Note: Honey should not be given to children under the age of 1 year.

Makes two 1 1/4-cup servings.

INGREDIENTS:

1 ripe banana
2 cups skim milk
1/3 cup fat-free cottage cheese
1 tablespoon honey
1 teaspoon vanilla extract
1 tablespoon chocolate syrup

WHAT YOU NEED:

Cutting board
Sharp knife
Blender
Measuring cups
Measuring spoons
Rubber spatula

NUTRIENT ANALYSIS PER 1 1/4 CUP SERVING:

Calories 230, carbohydrate 42g, protein 14g, fat 1g, saturated fat .5g, cholesterol 4mg, fiber 1.5g, sodium 258mg

FOOD EXCHANGES:
1 1/2 milk, 1 fruit, 1/2 starch

Hey, it's May! It's time to cook something up for mom. Try our Made for Mom Pie — a breakfast pie that will start her special day off right. Mom's not the only one to appreciate this month. Teacher Appreciation Week is the second week of May. Show your appreciation by making your teacher a Yak Snack favorite: Crunch-Munch Cookies.

The Yak loves getting out to spring festivals, including Cinco de Mayo, a May 5 celebration of Mexican independence. You can celebrate at home with Quesadilla Appetizers or with Nachos.

It's also National Salad Month and National Egg Month. You can work recipes for either salads or eggs into your May menus.

Photo by Kent Phillips

Made for Mom Breakfast Pie

INGREDIENTS:

1/2 cup sliced mushrooms
2 medium onions
1 small green bell pepper
Vegetable oil cooking spray
1/2 pound cooked, cubed
extra-lean ham
8 egg whites
2 ounces (1/2 cup)
shredded part-skim
mozzarella cheese
2 ounces (1/2 cup)
shredded fat-free cheddar
cheese
3/4 cup skim milk
Dash freshly ground black
pepper

WHAT YOU NEED:

Cutting board
Sharp knife
Chopping knife
Measuring cups
9-inch round pan
Wire whisk
Oven mitts
Medium bowl
Wire cooling rack

HOW YOU MAKE:

1. Chop onion and green pepper (see glossary).

2. Preheat oven to 375 degrees Fahrenheit.

3. Spray a 9-inch round pan with vegetable oil cooking spray.

4. Spread ham over bottom of pan. Top evenly with mushrooms, onion and green pepper.

5. In a medium bowl, whisk together the egg white, mozzarella cheese, cheddar cheese, skim milk and pepper.

6. Pour over the vegetables in the pan.

7. Bake for 45 minutes, or until knife inserted in center comes out clean.

8. Using oven mitts, remove from oven and place on wire cooling rack.

Makes 6 servings.

NUTRIENT ANALYSIS PER SERVING:

Calories 130, carbohydrate 6g, protein 18g, fat 4g, saturated fat 1.5g, cholesterol 24mg, fiber 0.5g, sodium 776mg

FOOD EXCHANGES:
1 vegetable, 2 lean meat

MAY

Quesadilla Appetizers

HOW YOU MAKE:

1. Spray a 10-inch skillet with vegetable oil cooking spray and heat over medium heat.

2. When hot, place one flour tortilla in skillet.

3. Top with approximately 3 tablespoons of the shredded cheese.

4. Place another flour tortilla on top of cheese.

5. Cook approximately 2 minutes. Then flip tortilla with a spatula and cook the other side for approximately 2 minutes or until very lightly browned.

6. Remove from pan with spatula and place on cutting board.

7. Repeat with the rest of the tortillas and cheese.

8. With a sharp knife, cut each tortilla into six pieces and arrange on a platter or in a large basket.

9. Serve immediately with the salsa.

Cook's Note: You can reheat the quesadillas before serving them by placing them in a single layer on a baking sheet and baking them at 400 degrees Fahrenheit for 4 to 5 minutes.

Makes 30 appetizers.

INGREDIENTS:

Vegetable oil cooking spray
10 (8-inch) flour tortillas
4 ounces shredded Monterey Jack cheese (low-fat)
2 cups salsa

WHAT YOU NEED:

10-inch skillet
Spatula
Cutting board
Sharp knife
Measuring cups
Small bowl
Spoon
Platter or large basket

MAY

NUTRIENT ANALYSIS PER APPETIZER:

Calories 58, carbohydrate 8g, protein 2g, fat 2g, saturated fat 1g, cholesterol 2mg, fiber 0, sodium 155mg

FOOD EXCHANGES:
1/2 starch, 1/2 fat

Nachos

INGREDIENTS:

1 pound ground turkey breast
1/2 of 1.25 ounce package taco seasoning mix
8 ounces baked tortilla chips
4 ounces shredded mozzarella cheese, made with part skim milk
4 ounces shredded low-fat cheddar cheese
1/3 cup canned chopped green chilies
3/4 cups salsa
3/4 cup fat-free sour cream

WHAT YOU NEED:

Large skillet
Cookie sheet
Spatula
Measuring cups
Measuring spoons
Wooden spoon
Aluminum foil
Large slotted spoon

HOW YOU MAKE:

1. Preheat oven to 400 degrees Fahrenheit.

2. Using a wooden spoon, crumble the ground turkey breast and taco seasoning mix in a large skillet and cook until turkey is cooked through.

3. Line a cookie sheet with aluminum foil. Place tortilla chips on cookie sheet.

4. Remove turkey from skillet with large slotted spoon.

5. Sprinkle tortilla chips with ground turkey, mozzarella cheese, cheddar cheese and green chilies.

6. Bake about 4 minutes or until cheese is melted.

7. Remove from the oven and, using spoon, top with salsa and sour cream. Serve immediately.

Makes 8 servings.

Yak Fact

While healthy kids and adults can handle the extra sodium, babies and those with high blood pressure, heart failure or kidney disease need to limit the amount of sodium they eat.

NUTRIENT ANALYSIS PER SERVING:

Calories 279, carbohydrate 31g, protein 25g, fat 5g, saturated fat 2.5g, cholesterol 46mg, fiber 2.5g, sodium 707mg

FOOD EXCHANGES:
2 1/2 starch, 2 1/2 meat

MAY

Brain-Boosting Salad

HOW YOU MAKE:

1. On a cutting board, using a sharp knife, cut the broccoli into florets (see glossary).

2. Shred carrots (see glossary).

3. Chop red onion (see glossary).

4. In a medium mixing bowl, mix broccoli, carrots, onion, cheese, water chestnuts and almonds.

5. In a small bowl, using a rubber spatula, mix mayonnaise sugar and vinegar. Stir well.

6. Add the mayonnaise mixture to the broccoli mixture and toss gently.

7. Sprinkle with bacon bits and chill for one hour or longer.

Makes 8 servings.

INGREDIENTS:

1 1/2 pounds fresh broccoli
1 1/2 medium carrots
1/2 medium red onion
1 cup (4 ounces) fat-free shredded cheddar cheese
1/2 cup sliced water chestnuts
1/4 cup sliced almonds
1/2 cup low-fat mayonnaise
2 tablespoons sugar
2 teaspoons red wine vinegar
1/4 cup bacon bits

WHAT YOU NEED:

Cutting board
Sharp knife
Shredder
Chopping knife
Measuring cups
Measuring spoons
Medium mixing bowl
Small mixing bowl
Large spoon
Rubber spatula

NUTRIENT ANALYSIS PER SERVING

Calories 167, carbohydrate 14g, protein 9g, fat 9g, saturated fat 0.5g, cholesterol 0, fiber 5g, sodium 351mg

FOOD EXCHANGES:
2 vegetables, 1/2 starch, 1/2 meat, 1 1/2 fat

MAY

Seven-Layer Salad

MAY

INGREDIENTS:

2 medium stalks celery, washed, ends removed
1 cup radishes
8 green onions
6 cups bite-size pieces of salad greens
6 tablespoons bacon bits
1 package (10 ounces) frozen green peas, thawed
1 cup non-fat plain yogurt
1 tablespoon low-fat mayonnaise
1/2 cup fat-free grated Parmesan cheese

WHAT YOU NEED:

Cutting board
Sharp knife
Measuring cups
Measuring spoons
Medium glass bowl
Rubber spatula
Small bowl
Large spoon
Salad tongs

HOW YOU MAKE:

1. On a cutting board, with a sharp knife, thinly slice the celery, radishes and green onion (see glossary).

2. Place the greens in a medium glass bowl.

3. Layer the celery, radishes, onions, bacon bits and peas on top of the greens.

4. In a small bowl, using rubber spatula, mix together the yogurt and mayonnaise.

5. Spread the mixture over the peas, covering the top completely and sealing it to the edge of the bowl. Sprinkle the top with the Parmesan cheese.

6. Cover and refrigerate for at least 2 hours but no longer than 12 hours to blend the flavors. Toss briefly before serving if desired.

Makes 6 servings.

NUTRIENT ANALYSIS PER SERVING:

Calories 173, carbohydrate 25g, protein 11g, fat 3g, saturated fat 0.5g, cholesterol 1mg, fiber 7g, sodium 433mg

FOOD EXCHANGES:
1 starch, 2 vegetable, 1/2 fat

Crunch Munch Cookies

MAY

HOW YOU MAKE:

1. Preheat oven to 375 degrees Fahrenheit.

2. In a medium bowl, using large spoon, mix together flour, baking powder and baking soda; set aside.

3. In a large mixing bowl, blend the oil with the sugar and brown sugar. With a hand mixer or wire whisk, beat in the egg whites and vanilla. Scrape sides with rubber spatula.

4. Add the flour mixture, cereal and chocolate chips, mixing until just blended.

5. Drop by teaspoonfuls on ungreased baking sheet, about 2 inches apart.

6. Bake for 10 minutes; do not overbake. Cookies will puff up and then flatten.

7. Remove from oven and cool slightly on the baking sheet, then remove to a wire rack to cool completely.

Makes 24 cookies.

INGREDIENTS:

1 cup unsifted all-purpose flour
1/2 teaspoon baking powder
1/2 teaspoon baking soda
1/4 cup canola oil
1/2 cup granulated sugar
1/2 cup brown sugar, firmly packed
2 egg whites
1 teaspoon vanilla
1 cup fruit-nut-flake cereal, such as Just Right or Basic 4
1/4 cup chocolate chips

WHAT YOU NEED:

Medium bowl
Large spoon
Large bowl
Rubber spatula
Wire whisk or hand mixer
Teaspoon
Baking sheet
Wire rack
Measuring cups
Measuring spoons
Oven mitts

NUTRIENT ANALYSIS PER COOKIE:

Calories 91, carbohydrate 16g, protein 1g, fat 3g, saturated fat 0.5g, cholesterol 0, fiber 0.5g, sodium 54mg

FOOD EXCHANGES:
1 starch, 1/2 fat

JUNE

School's out so you'll have more time to play — outside and in the kitchen. Everybody's in the mood for easy eating and take-along food to pack for picnics at the park or beach.

The Yak loves picnics — it's easy to invite a bunch of pals over when everybody brings a dish to share. You'll want to share the Yak's recipe for a Fuzzy Cheese Man (it's really a cheese ball) to eat with your favorite crackers or chips. (If you want, make the Fuzzy Cheese Man to look like your dad for Father's Day. He can snack on it as you make Dad's Sloppy Joes.)

June has much more going on as summer officially begins. Get off to a fruit-tastic start with our healthy, delicious Fruit Dip.

55

Dad's Sloppy Joes

JUNE

INGREDIENTS:

1 small onion
1 stalk celery
8 ounces ground turkey breast
8 ounces lean ground beef
6 ounce can tomato paste
1/4 cup catsup
1 tablespoon prepared mustard
1 tablespoon vinegar
1 tablespoon sugar
1 can (10 3/4 ounces) chicken gumbo soup concentrate
1 tablespoon barbecue sauce
8 hamburger buns

WHAT YOU NEED:

Cutting board
Sharp knife
Large skillet
Wooden spoon
Spatula
Measuring cups
Measuring spoons

HOW YOU MAKE:

1. Using sharp knife, chop onions and celery (see glossary).

2. In a large skillet over medium heat, brown the ground turkey and ground beef, stirring with wooden spoon.

3. Drain the fat.

4. Add the onion and celery to the meat mixture and cook, stirring occasionally, until soft, about 5 minutes.

5. Add tomato paste, catsup, mustard, vinegar, sugar, chicken gumbo soup concentrate and barbecue sauce. Bring to a boil. Reduce the heat and simmer 5 to 10 minutes.

6. Serve on hamburger buns.

Makes 8 servings.

Yak Fact . . . .

Did you know thiamin...
✪ helps the body use energy and helps keep the nervous system healthy.

Did you know niacin...
✪ helps the body use energy and promotes healthy skin, nerves and digestive tract.

NUTRIENT ANALYSIS PER SLOPPY JOE:

Calories 286, carbohydrate 35g, protein 18g, fat 8g, saturated fat 2.5g, cholesterol 40mg, fiber 3g, sodium 899mg

FOOD EXCHANGES:
2 starch, 1 vegetable, 1 1/2 meat

Oven-Baked French Fries

HOW YOU MAKE:

1. Preheat oven to 475 degrees Fahrenheit.

2. Cut each potato into half-inch strips, or make them thicker if you prefer more of a potato wedge.

3. Lightly spray a baking sheet with vegetable oil cooking spray.

4. Working in two batches, arrange potato strips in a single layer on baking sheet. Spray strips with vegetable oil cooking spray before placing pan in oven.

5. Bake the strips 15 to 20 minutes. Using oven mitts, turn them with spatula and continue baking until crisp and browned, approximately 15 to 20 more minutes (more for thicker wedges).

6. Using oven mitts, remove from oven.

Makes 6 servings.

INGREDIENTS:

6 large russet or other baking potatoes, scrubbed
Vegetable oil cooking spray

WHAT YOU NEED:

Cutting board
Sharp knife
Baking sheet
Spatula

JUNE

NUTRIENT ANALYSIS PER SERVING:

Calories 220, carbohydrate 51g, protein 5g, fat 0, saturated fat 0, cholesterol 0, fiber 4.5g, sodium 16mg

FOOD EXCHANGES:
3 1/2 starch

Fruit and Cheese Pockets

JUNE

INGREDIENTS:

1 large pita bread
1/2 cup fat-free cottage cheese
1/2 cup (2 ounces) shredded mozzarella cheese made from part-skim milk
One 8 3/4-ounce can of fruit cocktail, drained (no sugar added)
2 tablespoons sliced almonds
1 to 2 tablespoons skim milk (optional)
Lettuce leaves

WHAT YOU NEED:

Cutting board
Sharp knife
Small bowl
Strainer
Measuring cups
Measuring spoons

HOW YOU MAKE:

1. On a cutting board, with a sharp knife, cut a large pita bread crosswise.

2. In a small bowl, stir together cottage cheese, shredded mozzarella cheese, fruit cocktail and sliced almonds.

3. Add enough milk to moisten, if necessary; mix well.

4. Line the two pita pockets with lettuce.

5. Divide the fruit and cheese mixture evenly into the two pockets.

Cook's Note: You can make the mixture ahead of time and store it up to one week in an airtight container in the refrigerator. Small children may prefer to eat the mixture from the container and eat the pita bread separately.

Makes 2 sandwiches.

Yak Fact

Fruits and vegetables help supply your body with water.

NUTRIENT ANALYSIS PER SANDWICH:

Calories 305, carbohydrate 37g, protein 19g, fat 9g, saturated fat 3.5g, cholesterol 16mg, fiber 3g, sodium 558mg

FOOD EXCHANGES:
1 1/2 starch, 1 fruit, 2 meat

Strawberry Power Shake

HOW YOU MAKE:

1. Place the yogurt, strawberries, skim milk and honey in a blender.

2. Blend on medium speed.

3. Stop blender and scrape sides with rubber spatula.

4. Continue blending, if necessary, until smooth and frothy.

5. Pour into 4 glasses, using rubber spatula to scrape if necessary.

Makes four 1-cup servings.

Cook's Note: Children under the age of 1 should not eat honey.

INGREDIENTS:

16 ounces vanilla non-fat yogurt
1 cup frozen hulled strawberries
2 cups skim milk
2 tablespoons honey

WHAT YOU NEED:

Measuring cups
Measuring spoons
Blender
Rubber spatula

JUNE

NUTRIENT ANALYSIS PER CUP:

Calories 133, carbohydrate 25g, protein 8g, fat 0, saturated fat 0, cholesterol 5mg, fiber 1g, sodium 134mg

FOOD EXCHANGES:
1 milk, 1 fruit

Fuzzy Cheese Man

INGREDIENTS:

8 ounces fat-free block
cream cheese, softened
1 1/4 cup finely shredded
fat-free cheddar cheese
(about 5 ounces), divided
1 teaspoon Dijon mustard
1 teaspoon Worcestershire
sauce
1/2 teaspoon dried minced
onion
2 green olive halves
1 red pepper strip
2 baked tortilla chips or 2
low fat crackers

WHAT YOU NEED:

Medium bowl
Rubber spatula
Wax paper
Measuring cups
Measuring spoons

HOW YOU MAKE:

1. In a medium bowl, mix
together the cream cheese,
1 cup of cheddar cheese,
Dijon mustard,
Worcestershire sauce and
the minced onion. Place in
refrigerator for 2 hours.

2. Remove from refrigerator
and shape the cheese
mixture into a ball on waxed
paper.

3. Place remaining 1/4 cup of
cheddar cheese on waxed
paper; roll cheese ball in the
cheese.

4. Make a face using the
olives for eyes, red pepper
strip for mouth and baked
tortilla chips or crackers for
ears.

5. Serve with low-fat
crackers or baked tortilla
chips.

Makes twenty 1-tablespoon
servings.

NUTRIIENT ANALYSIS PER 1 TABLESPOON SERVING:

Calories 23, carbohydrate 2g, protein 3g, fat 0, saturated
fat 0, cholesterol 1mg, fiber 0g, sodium 142mg

FOOD EXCHANGES:
1/2 lean meat

Crispy Veggie Bake

HOW YOU MAKE:

1. Preheat oven to 400 degrees Fahrenheit.

2. With a vegetable peeler, peel the carrot, cut off ends.

3. On a cutting board, with a sharp knife, slice the carrot into 1/4-inch rounds and slice the zucchini into 2-inch slices.

4. In a small bowl, mix dry instant mashed potatoes, Parmesan cheese, garlic powder and basil leaves.

5. In a shallow dish beat egg substitute with a fork or small whisk.

6. Using a slotted spoon, dip broccoli into egg substitute. Roll broccoli in potato and cheese mixture.

7. Put broccoli on cookie sheet.

8. Repeat with all of the vegetables.

9. Bake 10 to 12 minutes or until light brown, turning once during baking using oven mitt and large spoon.

10. Immediately remove vegetables from cookie sheet with spatula and place on a serving plate.

Makes four 1/2-cup servings.

INGREDIENTS:

1 medium carrot (washed)
1/2 zucchini (washed and ends removed)
1/2 cup broccoli florets
1/2 cup cauliflower florets
1/2 cup dry instant mashed potatoes
1/4 cup fat-free grated Parmesan cheese
1/2 teaspoon garlic powder
1/4 teaspoon dried basil leaves
1/4 cup fat-free egg substitute (or more as needed)

WHAT YOU NEED:

Vegetable peeler
Cutting board
Sharp knife
Small bowls
Shallow dish
Slotted spoon
Cookie sheet
Measuring cups and spoons
Fork or short whisk
Spatula
Oven mitts

NUTRIENT ANALYSIS PER 1/2-CUP SERVING:

Calories 146, carbohydrate 30g, protein 5g, fat trace, saturated fat trace, cholesterol 0mg, fiber 3g, sodium 167mg

FOOD EXCHANGES:
1 1/2 starch, 1 vegetable

Fruit Dip

INGREDIENTS:

4 large carambola (star fruit), or 2 cups in-season favorite fruit such as whole strawberries, sliced nectarines
1 cup (8 ounces) non-fat vanilla yogurt
3 tablespoons orange marmalade
1 tablespoon confectioners' sugar

WHAT YOU NEED:

Cutting board
Sharp knife
Small bowl
Rubber spatula
Measuring cups
Measuring spoons

HOW YOU MAKE:

1. On a cutting board, using a sharp knife, slice and seed 4 large carambola (star fruit).

2. In a small bowl, using a rubber spatula, combine yogurt, marmalade and confectioners' sugar.

3. Serve with sliced star fruit or small whole fruits or fruit slices.

Makes 4 servings.

Yak Fact . . . .

Vitamins don't provide energy, but they do help your body process the energy you get from foods.

NUTRIENT ANALYSIS PER SERVING:

Calories 97, carbohydrate 22g, protein 3g, fat 0, saturated fat 0, cholesterol 1mg, fiber 3g, sodium 45mg

FOOD EXCHANGES:
1 fruit, 1/2 milk

JUNE

Marshmallow Fruit Dip

HOW YOU MAKE:

1. In a small bowl, using a hand mixer, whip cream cheese until smooth.

2. Stir in yogurt and marshmallow creme. Scrape sides of bowl.

3. Serve with your favorite cut-up fruit.

Makes sixteen 1-tablespoon servings.

INGREDIENTS:

1/4 cup lowfat block cream cheese, softened
1/4 cup non-fat vanilla yogurt
1/2 cup marshmallow creme

WHAT YOU NEED:

Hand mixer
Small bowl
Measuring cups
Rubber spatula

NUTRIENT ANALYSIS PER 1-TABLESPOON SERVING:

Calories 41, carbohydrate 8g, protein 1g, fat 1g, saturated fat 0.5g, cholesterol 2mg, fiber 0g, sodium 14mg

FOOD EXCHANGES:
1/2 starch

Strawberry Shortcake

INGREDIENTS:

1 quart fresh strawberries, washed
1 tablespoon plus 2 teaspoons sugar, divided
1 1/2 cup all-purpose flour, divided
1 teaspoon baking powder
1/8 teaspoon baking soda
1/3 cup buttermilk
2 tablespoons canola oil
1 cup non-fat vanilla yogurt
1 tablespoon brown sugar

WHAT YOU NEED:

Cutting board
Sharp knife
Large bowl
Large mixing spoon
Sifter
Medium mixing bowl
Small mixing bowl
2 rubber spatulas
Large spoon
Rolling pin
Biscuit cutter
Baking sheet
Long serrated knife
Measuring cups
Measuring spoons
Oven mitts

HOW YOU MAKE:

1. Slice the strawberries.

2. Preheat oven to 450 degrees Fahrenheit.

3. Place strawberries in a large bowl and sprinkle with 1 tablespoon sugar. Using a large mixing spoon, toss to coat and set aside.

4. In a medium bowl, sift together 1 cup flour, baking powder, baking soda and remaining 2 teaspoons sugar. Set aside.

5. In a small bowl, using rubber spatula, stir together buttermilk and oil. Pour over flour mixture; stir well.

6. Sprinkle work surface with remaining flour. Knead dough gently on floured surface for 10 to 12 strokes.

7. Roll or pat dough to half-inch thickness. Using a 2-inch biscuit cutter, dipping cutter in flour between cuts, cut eight biscuits. Using spatula, transfer biscuits to an ungreased baking sheet.

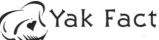 Yak Fact •••••••••••••••••

Some people eat a lot of different foods, but they eat too much. The extra food turns to fat. Eat desserts in moderation.

JUNE

8. Bake in oven for 10 to 12 minutes or until golden.

9. In a small bowl, using rubber spatula, mix the yogurt and brown sugar.

10. Remove the biscuits from the oven using oven mitts.

11. Using a long serrated knife, on a large cutting board cut each of the biscuits in half lengthwise. Using large spoon, divide half of the strawberries up between the layers.

Replace the top half of the biscuit and spoon the remaining strawberries on top of the biscuit.

12. Divide the yogurt sauce up evenly and place on top of the strawberries.

Makes 8 servings.

NUTRIENT ANALYSIS PER SERVING:

Calories 172, carbohydrate 30g, protein 5g, fat 4g, saturated fat 0.5g, cholesterol 1mg, fiber 2g, sodium 101mg

FOOD EXCHANGES:
1 1/2 starch, 1/2 fruit, 1 fat

JUNE

JULY

Cooking in July is a blast. Celebrate your independence in the kitchen with Fourth of July Fruit Sparklers. This berry yummy treat is made with one of the Yak's favorite fruits: blueberries. (By the way, it's National Blueberry Month.) Our country isn't the only one celebrating. The French celebrate their independence on Bastille Day, July 14. You can serve up Zesty French Bread on that day — or any day.

July continues what June began — more outside eating. Help make a burger that can't be beat. Get stuffed with Stuffed Burgers, a healthy surprise.

Photo by Kent Phillips

Fancy Fruit Salad

INGREDIENTS:

2 kiwi
1/2 cup non-fat lemon yogurt
2 tablespoons low-fat mayo-type dressing
2 teaspoons light brown sugar
1 teaspoon grated lemon peel
1/4 teaspoon ground ginger
Dash salt
3 cups canned or jarred tropical fruit mix (pineapple, mango, papaya)
1 tablespoon slivered almonds

WHAT YOU NEED:

Cutting board
Sharp knife
Small bowl
Rubber spatula
Medium bowl
Measuring cups
Measuring spoons

HOW YOU MAKE:

1. On a cutting board, using a sharp knife, pare and cube the kiwi.

2. In a small bowl, blend together yogurt, dressing, sugar, lemon peel, ginger and salt. Cover and chill at least 30 minutes.

3. Place the tropical fruit and kiwi in a medium size bowl.

4. Pour dressing mix on top of fruit and sprinkle with the almonds.

Makes six 1/2-cup servings.

NUTRIENT ANALYSIS PER 1/2-CUP SERVING:

Calories 109, carbohydrate 22g, protein 2g, fat 2g, saturated fat 0, cholesterol trace, fiber 2.5g, sodium 109mg

FOOD EXCHANGES:
1 1/2 fruit, 1/2 fat

JULY

July Fourth Fruit Sparklers

HOW YOU MAKE:

1. Using sharp knife, slice strawberries on cutting board.

2. Reserve one of the strawberry slices for garnish.

3. In a small bowl, using a fork, mix the remaining strawberries and sugar together. Mix well, mashing a few of the berries as you mix.

4. Using a spoon, put the strawberry mixture into the bottom of a parfait glass.

5. Top the strawberries with a scoop of the vanilla ice cream.

6. Reserve one blueberry for garnish, then top the ice cream with the remaining blueberries.

7. Top the final layer of blueberries with the fat-free frozen whipped topping and garnish with the reserved strawberry slice and blueberry.

Cook's Note: You can make this ahead. Put the special glasses in the freezer. Then fill the glasses as directed above, except for the whipped topping and garnish, and return to the freezer for a few hours until you are ready to serve. Add the whipped topping and garnish right before you serve your parfaits.

Makes 1 serving.

INGREDIENTS:

1/4 cup fresh strawberries
1 teaspoon sugar
1/2 cup fat-free vanilla ice cream
2 tablespoons fresh blueberries
2 tablespoons fat-free whipped topping

WHAT YOU NEED:

Cutting board
Sharp knife
Small bowl
Fork
Spoon
Measuring cups
Measuring spoons
Parfait glass (tall fancy glass)
Ice cream scoop

JULY

NUTRIENT ANALYSIS PER SERVING:

Calories 151, carbohydrate 34g, protein 3g, fat 0, saturated fat 0, cholesterol 0, fiber 1.5g, sodium 51mg

FOOD EXCHANGES:
1 fruit, 1 starch

Zesty French Bread

INGREDIENTS:

2 teaspoons fresh parsley, packed
4 (1-ounce) slices french bread, toasted
4 teaspoons low-fat Italian dressing, divided
2 ounces (1/2 cup) shredded part-skim Mozzarella cheese

WHAT YOU NEED:

Cutting board
Sharp knife
Pastry brush
Measuring spoons
Broiler rack
Cooling rack
Oven mitts

HOW YOU MAKE:

1. Using a cutting board and a sharp knife, mince fresh parsley.

2. Place toasted bread slices on a broiler pan.

3. Using a pastry brush, brush top side of each bread slice lightly with salad dressing.

4. Sprinkle cheese and parsley evenly over bread slices.

5. Broil 6 inches from heat until cheese melts.

6. Using oven mitts, remove from oven and set on cooling rack. Serve immediately.

Makes 4 servings.

Yak Fact • • • • • • • • • • • • •

It's best to take in enough calories to keep your body growing without adding too much extra padding.

NUTRIENT ANALYSIS PER SERVING:

Calories 110, carbohydrate 14g, protein 6g, fat 3g, saturated fat 1.5g, cholesterol 8mg, fiber 1g, sodium 257mg

FOOD EXCHANGES:
1 starch

Creamy Coleslaw

HOW YOU MAKE:

1. On a cutting board, with a sharp knife, chop green onion (see glossary).

2. In a large bowl, place the shredded coleslaw vegetables. Add lemon juice and green onion and toss gently.

3. In a small bowl, mix together the yogurt, mayonnaise, celery seed, sugar and pepper.

4. Pour yogurt mixture over coleslaw. Add raisins and walnuts. Mix well.

Serve immediately or cover and chill.

Makes twelve 3/4-cup servings.

INGREDIENTS:

1 green onion
16-ounce package shredded coleslaw vegetables
1 to 2 tablespoons lemon juice
1/2 cup non-fat plain yogurt
1/2 cup low-fat mayonnaise
1/2 teaspoon celery seed
1/2 teaspoon sugar
1/4 teaspoon freshly ground white pepper
1/4 cup raisins
2 tablespoons chopped walnuts

WHAT YOU NEED:

Cutting board
Sharp knife
Large bowl
Mixing spoon
Small bowl
Rubber spatula
Measuring cups
Measuring spoons

JULY

NUTRIENT ANALYSIS PER 3/4-CUP SERVING:

Calories 66, carbohydrate 7g, protein 1g, fat 4g, saturated fat 0.5g, cholesterol trace, fiber 1g, sodium 83mg

FOOD EXCHANGES:
1 vegetable, 1 fat

Stuffed Burgers

INGREDIENTS:

1 pound extra-lean ground beef
1 pound ground turkey breast
6 slices fat-free cheddar cheese
1 medium green pepper
1 medium onion
1 medium tomato
Black pepper
Lettuce leaves
6 hamburger buns

WHAT YOU NEED:

Large bowl
Cutting board
Knife
Large spoon

HOW YOU MAKE:

1. Turn on the broiler or preheat the grill.

2. Core and julienne the pepper (see glossary). Peel onion and slice into 6 rings. (Do not separate the rings.) Cut tomato into 6 slices.

3. In a large bowl, mix together the ground beef and turkey breast. Shape the meat mixture into 12 thin patties. Top six of the patties with slices of cheese, green pepper strips and the onion and tomato slices. Top each of those patties with one of the remaining patties and press the edges together to seal in the stuffing. Season with black pepper to taste.

4. Broil or grill the burgers until cooked through and the meat is no longer pink. Serve on lettuce-lined buns.

Makes 6 burgers.

 Yak Fact · · · · · · · · · · · · ·

Zinc is a mineral that is important for wound healing, proper immune function, protein metabolism and growth.

NUTRIENT ANALYSIS PER SERVING:

Calories 393, carbohydrate 28g, protein 42g, fat 12g, saturated fat 4g, cholesterol 108mg, fiber 2g, sodium 489 mg

FOOD EXCHANGES:
2 starch, 5 lean meat

Grape Fizz

HOW YOU MAKE:

1. On a cutting board, with a sharp knife, slice lime into 8 slices.

2. Place lime slice in each of 8 glasses.

3. In a pitcher, mix club soda and grape juice.

4. Pour one cup of mixture over each lime slice and serve.

Makes 8 one-cup servings.

INGREDIENTS:

1 lime
5 cups club soda, chilled
3 cups unsweetened grape juice

WHAT YOU NEED:

Cutting board
Sharp knife
8 glasses
Pitcher
Measuring cups

Yak Fact • • • •

Have you noticed that your mouth starts to feel dry and sticky when you haven't had a drink for a while? This is your body's way of telling you it needs water.

NUTRIENT ANALYSIS PER CUP:

Calories 59, carbohydrate 15g, protein 1g, fat 0, saturated fat 0, cholesterol 0, fiber 0.5g, sodium 34mg

FOOD EXCHANGES:
1 fruit

AUGUST

Ah, August. Time for the last bit of vacation fun before heading back to school. It's Friendship Day on the first Monday in August. You can bake your buddy some of our S'more Fun Snack Cake, bringing back memories of summer camp.

Sweet corn is ripe in the fields and that calls for something corny. The simplest way to cook corn is to boil or steam it. Or you can do something some folks love in Iowa — where corn is a major crop. Got milk? Got corn? Get cooking.

When the August heat can't be beat, try a Frozen Banana Pop. It's cool to make and cool to eat.

Photo by Kent Phillips

Frozen Banana Pops

INGREDIENTS:

2 large bananas
1/2 cup non-fat strawberry yogurt
1 cup crispy rice cereal

WHAT YOU NEED:

Table knife
4 wooden sticks
Small shallow bowl
Plate
Measuring cups

HOW YOU MAKE:

1. Peel and cut bananas crosswise in half with a table knife.

2. Carefully poke a wooden stick into the cut end of each banana half.

3. Using rubber spatula, put yogurt in shallow bowl.

4. Roll each banana half in the yogurt, then sprinkle with the crispy rice cereal.

5. Put banana halves on plate.

6. Place plate in freezer and freeze about 2 hours or until hard. Keep frozen until ready to serve.

Makes 4 servings.

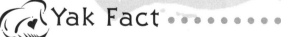

Yak Fact · · · · · · · ·

You need five servings of fruits and vegetables every day.

NUTRIENT ANALYSIS PER SERVING:

Calories 93, carbohydrate 22g, protein 2g, fat 0, saturated fat 0, cholesterol 1mg, fiber 1.5g, sodium 83mg

FOOD EXCHANGES:
1 fruit, 1/2 starch

AUGUST

Hearty Party Mix

HOW YOU MAKE:

1. Preheat oven to 250 degrees Fahrenheit.

2. In a large baking dish, combine the toasted oat cereal, Rice Chex, Wheat Chex, peanuts and pretzel sticks and twists. Set aside.

3. In a small bowl, using a wire whisk, whisk together canola oil, Worcestershire sauce, garlic powder, paprika and ground red pepper. Pour over cereal mixture. Stir with wooden spoon to coat.

4. Place pan in oven and bake for one hour stirring every 15 minutes.

5. Using oven mitts, remove from oven and let cool to room temperature.

6. Store in airtight container.

Makes twenty 2/3-cup servings.

INGREDIENTS:

3 cups toasted oat cereal
3 cups Rice Chex
2 cups Wheat Chex
1/4 cup peanuts
2 cups pretzel sticks
2 cups pretzel twists
1/4 cup canola oil
1 tablespoon Worcestershire sauce
1 teaspoon garlic powder
1/2 teaspoon paprika
1/4 teaspoon ground red (cayenne) pepper

WHAT YOU NEED:

1 large baking pan
Small bowl
Wire whisk
Oven mitts
Wooden spoon
Measuring cups
Measuring spoons
Airtight container or large zippered plastic bag

AUGUST

NUTRIENT ANALYSIS PER SERVING:

Calories 121, carbohydrate 19g, protein 2g, fat 4g, saturated fat 0.5g, cholesterol 0, fiber 1.5g, sodium 276mg

FOOD EXCHANGES:
1 starch, 1 fat

Blueberry Pancakes

AUGUST

INGREDIENTS:

1 cup all-purpose flour
1 teaspoon sugar
3/4 teaspoon baking powder
1/4 teaspoon salt
2 egg whites
1 cup low-fat buttermilk
1 tablespoon canola oil
1 cup blueberries
Vegetable oil cooking spray

WHAT YOU NEED:

Medium bowl
Sifter
Small bowl
Wire whisk
Measuring cups
Measuring spoons
Skillet
Pancake turner

HOW YOU MAKE:

1. In a medium bowl, sift together flour, sugar, baking powder and salt and set aside.

2. In a small bowl, with a wire whisk, beat egg whites slightly.

3. Add buttermilk and oil and mix well with large spoon.

4. Add wet ingredients to the dry mixture, stirring just enough to combine.

5. Add blueberries and mix carefully.

6. Spray skillet with vegetable oil cooking spray and heat over medium heat.

7. Using measuring cup, pour batter into skillet, making pancakes approximately 3 to 4 inches in diameter.

8. Cook until bottoms are golden brown and bubbles on the top begin to break.

9. Flip over with a pancake turner and cook until golden brown.

10. Repeat until all batter is gone.

Makes 12 pancakes.

Yak Fact • • • • • • • •

The secret to making pancakes is getting the griddle hot enough.

NUTRIENT ANALYSIS PER 3 PANCAKES:

Calories 201, carbohydrate 33g, protein 7g, fat 4g, saturated fat 1g, cholesterol 2mg, fiber 2g, sodium 315mg

FOOD EXCHANGES:
2 starch, 1 fat

Blueberry Sauce

HOW YOU MAKE:

1. In a small saucepan, combine sugar and cornstarch.

2. Add blueberries, lemon juice and water.

3. Cook over medium heat, stirring until mixture thickens.

4. Remove from heat and serve over pancakes.

Makes 32 tablespoons.

INGREDIENTS:

1/3 cup sugar
1 tablespoon cornstarch
2 cups fresh or frozen blue-berries
2 tablespoons lemon juice
1/3 cup water

WHAT YOU NEED:

Small saucepan
Wooden spoon
Measuring cups
Measuring spoons

AUGUST

NUTRIENT ANALYSIS PER 2 TABLESPOONS:

Calories 34, carbohydrate 9g, protein 0, fat trace, saturated fat 0, cholesterol 0, fiber 0.5g, sodium 2mg

FOOD EXCHANGES:
. 1/2 fruit

S'more Snack Cake

INGREDIENTS:

Vegetable oil cooking spray plus 1 teaspoon flour or floured baking spray
1 cup all-purpose flour
2 cups graham cracker crumbs
1 teaspoon baking powder
1 teaspoon baking soda
1 cup firmly packed brown sugar
1/2 cup unsweetened applesauce
3/4 cup fat-free egg substitute
1 cup skim milk
1 cup miniature semi-sweet chocolate chips, divided
1 jar (3 ounce) or 1 1/2 cups marshmallow creme

WHAT YOU NEED:

13-inch by 9-inch baking pan
Medium bowl
Large spoon
Large bowl
Hand mixer
Rubber spatula
Measuring cups
Measuring spoons
Oven mitts
Cooling rack
Small saucepan
Wooden spoon
Teaspoon
Butter knife
Glass

HOW YOU MAKE:

1. Preheat oven to 350 degrees Fahrenheit.

2. Spray and flour 13-inch by 9-inch pan or spray it with floured baking spray.

3. In a medium bowl, combine flour, graham cracker crumbs, baking powder and baking soda. Mix well. Set aside.

4. In a large bowl, with a hand mixer, beat brown sugar, applesauce, egg substitute and skim milk until well blended. Beat at medium speed for 1 minute.

5. Stir in 2/3 cup of the chocolate chips.

6. Spread batter evenly in prepared pan.

7. Bake for 25 to 35 minutes until toothpick inserted in center comes out clean. Using oven mitts, remove from oven. Cool on cooling rack for 15 minutes.

8. Meanwhile, melt remaining 1/3 cup chocolate chips in small saucepan over low heat, stirring with wooden spoon.

9. Spoon teaspoonfuls of marshmallow creme onto top of warm cake.

10. Carefully spread marshmallow creme with knife dipped in glass of hot water.

11. Drizzle with melted chocolate and swirl chocolate through marshmallow creme to marble.

Makes 16 servings.

NUTRIENT ANALYSIS PER SERVING:

Calories 217, carbohydrate 41g, protein 4g, fat 5g, saturated fat 2.5g, cholesterol trace, fiber 1.5g, sodium 161mg

FOOD EXCHANGES:
3 starch, 1 fat

AUGUST

Oven-Fried Chicken

HOW YOU MAKE:

1. Preheat oven to 350 degrees Fahrenheit.

2. In a medium bowl, using a large spoon, mix bread crumbs, Parmesan cheese, oregano, basil and pepper.

3. Cover baking sheet with aluminum foil and spray with vegetable oil cooking spray.

4. Pour buttermilk into small bowl. Dip chicken breasts one at a time into buttermilk and roll in Parmesan mixture, shaking off excess.

5. Place chicken breasts on baking sheet and bake for 1 hour, turning after 30 minutes.

Makes 4 servings.

INGREDIENTS:

1/2 cup bread crumbs
2 tablespoons grated fat-free Parmesan cheese
1/2 teaspoon dried oregano
1/4 teaspoon dried basil
1/4 teaspoon pepper
1/2 cup low fat buttermilk
Four 4-ounce, boneless, skinless chicken breasts
Vegetable oil cooking spray

WHAT YOU NEED:

Medium bowl
Large spoon
Aluminum foil
Baking sheet
Small bowl
Measuring cups
Measuring spoons

Yak Fact • • • • • • • • • • • • • • •

Nutrients are the parts of foods that give you energy, help you grow and keep you healthy. You need to eat foods with different kinds of nutrients.

NUTRIENT ANALYSIS PER SERVING:

Calories 214, carbohydrate 12g, protein 30g, fat 4g, saturated fat 1g, cholesterol 75mg, fiber 0.5g, sodium 214mg

FOOD EXCHANGES:
1/2 starch, 4 lean meat

Corn on the Cob

INGREDIENTS:

1 dozen ears of corn
6 cups or more water, enough to cover
1 tablespoon sugar
2 to 3 cups skim milk, or to cover, at room temperature

WHAT YOU NEED:

Large pot
Measuring cups
Measuring spoons
Tongs

HOW YOU MAKE:

1. Husk the corn — that means removing the leafy green part and silky strands around the ear. Hint: It's a fun chore outside on the deck or patio. Then wash the corn.

2. Put water in large pot and add sugar. Heat to rolling boil over high heat.

3. Drop corn in water ear by ear so as not to disturb the boiling (you may have to cook corn in two batches). Reduce heat slightly, cover and cook for about five minutes. Drain water from pot, leaving corn in the pot.

4. Add milk. Cover and put pot on low heat to keep warm until ready to serve.

Makes 12 servings.

Yak Fact ·····················

Although you need salt, eating too much is bad for your heart. That's why it is best not to add any salt to your food at the table. There's enough salt already in your food.

NUTRIENT ANALYSIS PER SERVING:

Calories 120, carbohydrate 29g, protein 4g, fat 1g, saturated fat 0, cholesterol 0, fiber 2g, sodium 4 mg

FOOD EXCHANGE:
2 starch

Zippy Zucchini Bread

HOW YOU MAKE:

1. Shred zucchini.

2. Chop walnuts (see glossary).

3. Preheat oven to 350 degrees Fahrenheit.

4. Spray two 8 1/2-inch by 4 1/2-inch loaf pans with vegetable oil cooking spray.

5. In a large bowl, mix together the oil, applesauce and sugar.

6. Using a wire whisk, add the egg whites, two at a time, beating after each addition.

7. In a medium bowl, mix the flour, cocoa, baking powder, baking soda and cinnamon.

8. Add dry ingredients to wet ingredients alternately with the milk.

9. Stir in the zucchini and walnuts.

10. Divide mixture evenly between the two loaf pans.

11. Bake for 45-55 minutes or until a cake tester inserted in the center comes out clean.

12. Using oven mitts, remove from oven. Cool on wire cooling racks.

Makes 20 servings.

INGREDIENTS:

2 medium size zucchini
1 ounce walnuts
vegetable oil cooking spray
3 tablespoons canola oil
1/3 cup unsweetened applesauce
2 cups sugar
6 egg whites
2 1/2 cups sifted flour
1/2 cup unsweetened cocoa
2 1/2 teaspoons baking powder
1 1/2 teaspoons baking soda
1 teaspoon cinnamon
1/2 cup skim milk

WHAT YOU NEED:

Food processor or shredder
Cutting board
Sharp knife
Large bowl
Rubber spatula
Medium bowl
Wire whisk
Two 8 1/2-inch by 4 1/2-inch loaf pans
Large spoon
Measuring cups
Measuring spoons
Oven mitts
Cake tester
Cooling racks

NUTRIENT ANALYSIS PER SERVING:

Calories 169, carbohydrate 33g, protein 3g, fat 3g, saturated fat 0.5g, cholesterol trace, fiber 1g, sodium 165mg

FOOD EXCHANGES:
2 starch, 1/2 fat

AUGUST

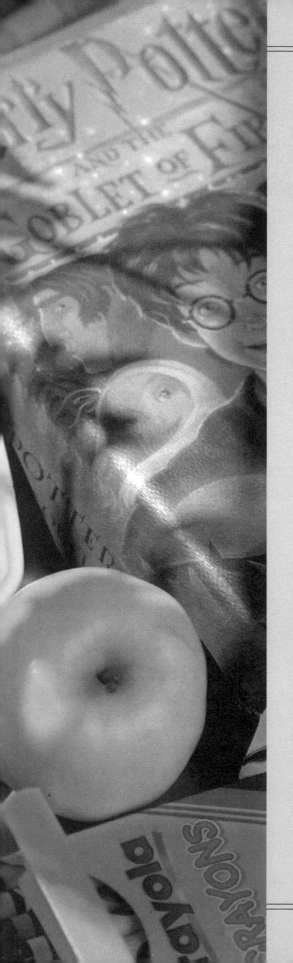

SEPTEMBER

Back to school means back to making school lunches. You can really help your parents by lending a hand in the kitchen. Check out our Pleasing Pita Pockets with your favorite lunch meat fillings.

Fall begins and there's a chill in the evening. Try our Pretend Pasta to warm up.

Some of you celebrate Rosh Hashanah, the Jewish New Year. Sweet apples and honey are served to express hopes for a sweet year ahead. Try our Apples 'N Honey recipe.

September is special — new beginnings, a new school year and new recipes to try.

85

Photo by Kent Phillips

Teddy Bear Snack Mix

INGREDIENTS:

3 cups teddy bear shaped graham snacks
1 cup raisins
1 cup chopped dried apples
1 cup honey nut round toasted oat cereal
1/4 cup candy-coated chocolate pieces (M & M type)

WHAT YOU NEED:

Large bowl
Large spoon
Large zippered plastic bag
Measuring cups

HOW YOU MAKE:

1. In a large bowl, mix teddy bear shaped graham snacks, raisins, dried apples, honey nut round oat cereal and candy-coated chocolate pieces.

2. Store snack mix in a sealed plastic bag or airtight container at room temperature up to 5 days.

Makes twelve 1/2-cup servings.

Yak Fact

Eating too much sugar leads to cavities in your teeth. Cavities need fillings and no one likes to get a filling. So don't forget to brush your teeth after snacking.

NUTRIENT ANALYSIS PER SERVING:

Calories 174, carbohydrate 33g, protein 2g, fat 4g, saturated fat 1g, cholesterol 0, fiber 2g, sodium 132mg

FOOD EXCHANGES:
1 starch, 1 fruit, 1 fat

SEPTEMBER

Pleasing Pita Pockets

HOW YOU MAKE:

1. Slice pita round in half.

2. Spread each half with spicy mustard.

3. Place 1 bologna slice, 1 cheese slice and lettuce leaf in each half.

Makes 2 servings.

INGREDIENTS:

1 eight-inch whole wheat pita round
4 teaspoons spicy mustard
2 low-fat bologna slices
2 fat-free American processed cheese slices
2 lettuce leaves

WHAT YOU NEED:

Cutting board
Sharp knife
Table knife
Measuring spoons

SEPTEMBER

NUTRIENT ANALYSIS PER SERVING:

Calories 186, carbohydrate 23g, protein 11g, fat 5g, saturated fat 1.5g, cholesterol 18mg, fiber 2.5g, sodium 886mg

FOOD EXCHANGES:
1 1/2 starch, 1 meat, 1/2 fat

Pretend Pasta

INGREDIENTS:

1 medium onion
1 small green pepper
1 large clove garlic
4 medium tomatoes
1 spaghetti squash
(about 1 1/2 pounds)
Vegetable oil cooking spray
1/2 teaspoon Italian
seasoning
1/8 teaspoon black pepper
1/4 cup grated fat-free
Parmesan cheese

WHAT YOU NEED:

Cutting board
Sharp knife
Fork
3-quart saucepan
Wooden spoon
Measuring cups
Measuring spoons
Large spoon
Large bowl

HOW YOU MAKE:

1. Chop onion, green pepper, garlic and tomatoes (see glossary).

2. Pierce whole squash in several places to allow steam to escape. Place on paper towel. Microwave uncovered 18 to 23 minutes, turning squash over after 8 minutes, until tender. Let stand uncovered 10 minutes.

3. Spray a 3-quart saucepan with vegetable oil cooking spray. In the saucepan, cook onion, green pepper and garlic over medium heat, about 5 minutes, stirring occasionally until onion is tender.

4. Stir in tomatoes, Italian seasoning and pepper. Simmer uncovered, stirring occasionally, 5 minutes.

5. On a cutting board, using a sharp knife, cut squash in half and remove seeds and fibrous strings. Remove squash strands with two forks and place in large bowl.

6. Toss strands with cheese. Spoon tomato mixture over squash. Serve.

Makes 6 servings.

NUTRIENT ANALYSIS PER SERVING:

Calories 73, carbohydrate 16g, protein 2g, fat 1g, saturated fat 0, cholesterol 0mg, fiber 3g, sodium 56mg

FOOD EXCHANGES:
1/2 starch, 1 vegetable, 1/2 fat

SEPTEMBER

Backpack Granola Bars

HOW YOU MAKE:

1. Chop dried fruit (see glossary).

2. Preheat oven to 300 degrees Fahrenheit.

3. In a large mixing bowl combine the oats, almonds and wheat germ; set aside.

4. In a small bowl, stir together honey and apple juice concentrate. Pour over oat mixture, stirring until coating is even.

5. Spray 9-inch by 13-inch baking pan with vegetable oil cooking spray. Spread mixture evenly into pan.

6. Bake uncovered for 45 to 40 minutes or until brown. Stir every 15 minutes and several times during the last 15 minutes. Using oven mitts, remove from oven.

7. Stir in raisins and dried fruit. Transfer to another pan and cool. Store in an airtight container.

Makes ten 1/2-cup servings.

Cook's Note: Children under the age of 1 year should not eat honey.

INGREDIENTS:

1/2 cup dried fruit (apples, apricots, or any other dried fruit)
2 1/2 cups rolled oats
1/2 cup slivered almonds
1/2 cup wheat germ
1/4 cup honey
1/3 cup frozen apple juice concentrate
Vegetable oil cooking spray
1/4 cup raisins

WHAT YOU NEED:

Cutting board
Sharp knife
Large mixing bowl
Wooden spoon
Small bowl
Small whisk
9-inch by 13-inch baking pan
Oven mitts

NUTRIENT ANALYSIS PER 1/2-CUP SERVING:

Calories 223, carbohydrate 39, protein 7g, fat 5g, saturated fat 0.5g, cholesterol 0, fiber 4.5g, sodium 5mg

FOOD EXCHANGES:
2 starch, 1/2 fruit, 1 fat

Microwave Cinnamon-Spiced Applesauce

INGREDIENTS:

6 medium McIntosh apples
1 teaspoon ground cinnamon
1/4 cup sugar

WHAT YOU NEED:

Cutting board
Peeler
Sharp knife
2-quart microwave-safe dish with top
Wooden spoon
Measuring cups
Measuring spoons
Large spoon

HOW YOU MAKE:

1. Peel, core and slice apples (see glossary).

2. In a 2-quart microwave-safe casserole dish, combine apples and cinnamon with wooden spoon. Cover tightly.

3. Microwave on 100 percent power (high), 8-9 minutes or until apples are tender. Stir several times during cooking.

4. Mash apples with large spoon to desired consistency.

5. Stir in sugar.

Makes four half-cup servings.

Yak Fact

It's hard to know exactly how much food you should eat, but if you're strong and healthy, you're probably eating the right amount.

NUTRIENT ANALYSIS PER HALF-CUP SERVING:

Calories 157, carbohydrate 41g, protein 0, fat 1g, saturated fat 0, cholesterol 0, fiber 1g, sodium 0

FOOD EXCHANGES:
2 1/2 fruit

SEPTEMBER

Sunday Salad

HOW YOU MAKE:

1. Chop pecans (see glossary) and toast them.

2. Place boneless, skinless chicken breasts in microwave-safe pan.

3. Microwave 8 to 10 minutes, rotating dish half-turn after 4 minutes. The chicken should no longer be pink when thickest piece is cut.

4. Set chicken aside and allow to cool.

5. Cut grapes in half.

6. Cube apples.

7. When chicken is cool, cut it into bite-size pieces.

8. In a medium bowl, mix together pecans, chicken pieces, mayonnaise, lemon juice, grapes and apples.

9. Chill and serve on a bed of lettuce.

Makes 4 servings.

Cook's Note: To toast pecans, sprinkle chopped pecans in an ungreased heavy skillet. Cook over medium-low heat about 5 minutes, stirring constantly with a wooden spoon.

INGREDIENTS:

1/4 cup pecans
4 four-ounce, boneless, skinless chicken breasts
1 cup fat-free mayonnaise or salad dressing
1 tablespoon lemon juice
1 cup seedless grapes
1 Granny Smith apple
1 Red Delicious apple
4 large lettuce leaves

WHAT YOU NEED:

Cutting board
Sharp knife
Microwave-safe baking pan
Paring knife
Medium bowl
Large spoon

NUTRIENT ANALYSIS PER SERVING:

Calories 295, carbohydrate 28g, protein 27 g, fat 8g, saturated fat 1.5 g, cholesterol 72mg, fiber 3g, sodium 546 mg

FOOD EXCHANGES:
2 fruit, 4 meat

Apples 'N Honey

INGREDIENTS:

1 pound challah bread (a type of egg bread that can be found at most large supermarkets and Jewish bakeries)
2 apples
1/2 cup honey

WHAT YOU NEED:

Cutting board
Paring knife
Measuring cups
Small bowl
A pretty plate

HOW YOU MAKE:

1. Core and slice apples (see glossary).

2. Cut challah bread into small pieces.

3. Put honey into bowl and put apples and bread on plate. Serve.

Makes 8 servings.

Cook's Note: Children under age 1 should not eat honey.

NUTRIENT ANALYSIS PER SERVING:

(2 ounces challah, 1/4 apple, 1 tablespoon honey)
Calories 254, carbohydrate 50g, protein 5g, fat 4g, saturated fat 1g, cholesterol 52mg, fiber 2.5g, sodium 281mg

FOOD EXCHANGES:
2 1/2 starch, 1 fruit, 1 fat

SEPTEMBER

Rice Pilaf

HOW YOU MAKE:

1. Chop small onion (see glossary).

2. Saute onion in canola oil in large skillet. Stir with wooden spoon.

3. Add vermicelli and brown.

4. Add rice and stir lightly until rice is crisp.

5. Pour in chicken broth, cover and steam over low heat for about 30 minutes.

Makes 6 one-half cup servings.

INGREDIENTS:

1 small onion
1 tablespoon canola oil
1/4 cup uncooked vermicelli
3/4 cup long grain rice
1 can (14 1/2 ounce) fat-free chicken broth

WHAT YOU NEED:

Chopping board
Sharp knife
Large skillet with lid
Wooden spoon
Measuring cups
Measuring spoons

SEPTEMBER

Yak Fact · · · · · · · · · · · · · · · ·

Carbohydrates are the major source of energy for powering your body. Starches and sugars are both types of carbohydrates.

NUTRIENT ANALYSIS PER SERVING:

Calories 123, carbohydrate 22g, protein 3g, fat 3g, saturated fat 0.5g, cholesterol 2mg, fiber 0.5g, sodium 51mg

FOOD EXCHANGES:
1 1/2 starch, 1/2 fat

OCTOBER

October is one of the Yak's favorite months. The Yak loves jumping in piles of leaves, seeing the colors change, going to soccer and football games and playing outside.

All that fun sure works up an appetite. And since it's National Pasta Month, the Yak enjoys healthy, hearty pasta dinners. Try making Super Spaghetti Casserole.

Of course, the Yak loves getting ready for Halloween, from dressing up to whipping up favorite treats.

You'll want to make Candy Corn Cupcakes and Jack-O'-Lanterns on a Stick. There's no trick to these treats.

Photo by Kent Phillips

Candy Corn Cupcakes

INGREDIENTS:

Cupcakes:
Vegetable oil cooking spray
Supermoist light devil's food cake mix (18.25-ounce box)
1/4 teaspoon baking soda
1 1/3 cup water
3 egg whites

Frosting:
Vanilla creamy deluxe light frosting (1-pound container)
4 drops orange food coloring

Decorations:
1/2 cup candy corn (72 pieces)
2 black licorice twists (8-10 inches each)

WHAT YOU NEED:

Baking paper cups
Muffin pans
Large bowl
Hand mixer
Small bowl
Oven mitts
Small rubber spatula
Wire rack
Measuring cups
Measuring spoons
Spatula

HOW YOU MAKE:

1. Preheat oven to 350 degrees Fahrenheit.

2. Spray cupcake pans with vegetable oil cooking spray or line with baking paper cups.

3. Using a hand mixer, in a large bowl, blend cake mix, baking soda, water and egg whites on low speed for 30 seconds. Then beat on medium speed for 2 minutes or 300 strokes by hand, scraping sides with rubber spatula.

3. Fill cupcake pans two-thirds full.

4. Bake 15-20 minutes. Remove from oven with oven mitts. Cool 10 minutes in pans on wire cooling rack. Remove from pans and cool completely on wire rack.

5. In a small bowl, mix food coloring and frosting until shade of orange you desire.

6. Using a small spatula, frost cooled cupcakes. Make pumpkin faces on the frosted cupcakes using the candy corn and licorice.

Makes 24 cupcakes.

Cook's note: You can get creative with other sprinkles and decorations, depending on your diet. The nutritional information is for the cakes using the decorations of licorice and candy corn.

Makes 24 cupcakes.

NUTRIENT ANALYSIS PER CUPCAKE:

Calories 170, carbohydrate 38g, protein 1g, fat 2g, saturated fat 0.5g, cholesterol 0, fiber 0.5g, sodium 254mg

FOOD EXCHANGES:
2 1/2 starch, 1/2 fat

Jack-O'-Lantern Cookie Sticks

HOW YOU MAKE:

1. Preheat oven to 350 degrees Fahrenheit.

2. In a large bowl, with rubber spatula, cream margarine and sugar together.

3. Add pumpkin, syrup, vanilla and egg whites and beat well.

4. In a medium bowl, combine flour, baking soda, baking powder and spices; mix with large spoon. Add to creamed mixture and mix well.

5. Spray cookie sheet with vegetable oil cooking spray.

6. Drop dough by two level tablespoonsful onto cookie sheet.

7. Insert a stick onto one side of cookie; insert an almond sliver into the opposite side of the cookie.

8. Press raisins into dough for eyes, nose and mouth.

9. Bake for 15 to 20 minutes. Remove from oven with oven mitts and place on wire cooling racks.

10. Cool completely on wire rack. Store tightly covered.

Makes 31 cookies.

INGREDIENTS:

1/2 cup soft tub margarine
1/3 cup sugar
1 cup canned pumpkin
1/3 cup maple syrup
1 teaspoon vanilla extract
2 egg whites
2 cups all-purpose flour
1 teaspoon baking powder
1/2 teaspoon baking soda
1 teaspoon ground cinnamon
1 teaspoon nutmeg
1/2 teaspoon ginger
31 almond slivers
3 tablespoons raisins
Vegetable oil cooking spray

WHAT YOU NEED:

Large bowl
Rubber spatula
Medium bowl
Large spoon
Cookie sheet
Tablespoon
31 flat wooden sticks
Measuring cups
Measuring spoons
Wire cooling racks
Oven mitts

OCTOBER

NUTRIENT ANALYSIS PER COOKIE:

Calories 82, carbohydrate 12g, protein 1g, fat 3g, saturated fat 0.5g, cholesterol 0, fiber 0.5g, sodium 76mg

FOOD EXCHANGE:
1 starch, 1/2 fat

Spicy Warm Cider

INGREDIENTS:

1 gallon apple cider
1 can (6 ounces) frozen concentrate orange juice
7 cinnamon sticks
1 1/2 teaspoons whole cloves
1 teaspoon whole allspice

WHAT YOU NEED:

Small soup pot
Cheesecloth
Kitchen string
Measuring spoons

HOW TO MAKE:

1. In a small soup pot, combine cider and frozen orange juice.

2. Place the cinnamon sticks, cloves and allspice in a double layer of cheesecloth, tied with kitchen string.

3. Lower the bag into the juice.

4. Slowly bring mixture to a boil. Then allow to simmer, covered, for 30 minutes to one hour over low heat.

5. Strain if not using a cheesecloth bag.

6. Serve the cider warm (it can be reheated).

Cook's Note: Unpasteurized cider may carry E. coli, a type of bacteria. By bringing the mixture to a slow boil, you can kill the bacteria, making the cider safe to drink.

Makes thirty 1/2-cup servings.

 Yak Fact • • • • • • • • • • • • • •

Did you know that you can eat water? Most foods have a lot of water in them. A cucumber, for example, is almost all water.

NUTRIENT ANALYSIS PER 1/2 CUP SERVING:

Calories 73, carbohydrate 18g, protein 0, fat trace, saturated fat 0, cholesterol 0, fiber 0, sodium 14mg

FOOD EXCHANGES:
1 fruit

OCTOBER

Spinach Potato Pancakes

HOW YOU MAKE:

1. Thaw and squeeze dry the spinach in colander.

2. Finely grate the onion.

3. In a blender, mix milk, nutmeg, flour and oil. Scrape sides with rubber spatula.

4. Pour mixture into a large bowl and add potatoes, egg, egg whites, sugar, spinach and onion; mix with large spoon.

5. Spray an electric skillet or griddle with vegetable oil cooking spray.

6. When it is hot, spoon on the pancake batter using small measuring cup.

7. Cook several minutes on each side or until pancakes are nicely browned, turning with pancake turner.

8. Spray skillet as it becomes necessary while cooking remaining pancakes.

Makes 12 pancakes.

INGREDIENTS:

1 10-ounce package frozen chopped spinach
1/2 medium onion
1 1/4 cup skim milk
1/8 teaspoon ground nutmeg
1 cup plus 1 tablespoon flour
2 tablespoons canola oil
1/2 pound fat-free hash browns
1 egg
4 egg whites
1/2 teaspoon sugar
Vegetable oil cooking spray

WHAT YOU NEED:

Colander
Grater
Blender
Rubber spatula
Large bowl
Large spoon
Electric skillet or griddle
Pancake turner
Measuring cups
Measuring spoons

NUTRIENT ANALYSIS PER PANCAKE:

Calories 98, carbohydrate 14g, protein 4g, fat 3g, saturated fat 0.5g, cholesterol 18mg, fiber 1.5g, sodium 64mg

FOOD EXCHANGES:
1 vegetable, 1/2 starch, 1/2 fat

OCTOBER

Microwave Spinach and Lasagna Roll-ups

INGREDIENTS:

1 medium onion
1 egg
6 lasagna noodles
1 10-ounce package frozen chopped spinach, thawed
1/2 pound lean ground beef
1 cup fat-free cottage cheese
1 teaspoon dried oregano, crushed
1 teaspoon dried basil, crushed
1 clove garlic, minced
1 15-ounce can tomato-herb sauce
1/4 cup grated fat-free Parmesan cheese

WHAT YOU NEED:

Cutting board
Sharp knife
Wire whisk
Small bowl
Sauce pan
Large wooden spoon
Colander
1 1/2 quart microwave-safe casserole dish
Large spoon
Large bowl
10-inch by 6-inch by 2-inch microwave-safe dish
Medium bowl
Rubber spatula
Oven mitts

HOW YOU MAKE:

1. On cutting board, with sharp knife, chop onion (see glossary).

2. In a small bowl, with a wire whisk, slightly beat the egg.

3. Cook noodles according to package directions, omitting the salt, and drain in colander.

4. Thoroughly drain spinach, pressing out excess liquid.

5. In a 1 1/2-quart microwave-safe casserole dish, cook spinach on 100 percent power (high) for 7 to 9 minutes or until done, stirring once. Drain.

6. Crumble beef into a microwave-safe casserole dish. Stir in onion. Microwave uncovered on 100 percent power (high) for 3 to 5 minutes or until beef is done, stirring twice to break up meat. Spoon off fat using large spoon.

Yak Fact

Starchy foods (potatoes, pasta, bread, etc.) provide valuable vitamins and minerals along with energy.

OCTOBER

7. In a medium bowl, stir together cottage cheese, egg, oregano, basil and garlic using rubber spatula.

8. Stir cottage cheese mixture and meat mixture into spinach.

9. Spread some spinach-meat mixture on each lasagna noodle.

10. Roll up jelly-roll style, starting with one short edge.

11. Place seam side down in a 10-inch by 6-inch by 2-inch microwave-safe baking dish.

12. Pour tomato-herb sauce over rolls.

14. Microwave, uncovered on 100 percent power (high) for 10-12 minutes or until heated through, rotating a half-turn twice. Remove using oven mitts.

15. Transfer to individual plate. Sprinkle some of the Parmesan cheese on each roll.

Makes 6 servings.

NUTRIENT ANALYSIS PER SERVING:

Calories 224, carbohydrate 13g, protein 21g, fat 10g, saturated fat 3.5g, cholesterol 108mg, fiber 3g, sodium 531mg

Yak Fact

Fiber, which helps move the food through your body and get rid of wastes, is found in many starchy foods, fruits, and vegetables.

Yak Fact

No wonder soda pop tastes sweet. A glassful can have about 5 teaspoons of sugar dissolved in it.

Yak Fact

Your heart pumps the blood through your body, taking nutrients from food to where they need to go.

Yak Fact

Your body makes vitamin D when the sun shines on your skin. That's why it is also called the sunshine vitamin.

OCTOBER

FOOD EXCHANGES:
1/2 starch, 1 vegetable, 2 1/2 meat

Pita Pizza Treats

INGREDIENTS:

1 medium onion
1/4 of medium zucchini
1 small green bell pepper
1 cup sliced mushrooms
Three 6 1/2-inch pita bread rounds
1 cup pizza sauce or spaghetti sauce
1 1/4 cups (5 ounces) shredded mozzarella cheese made from skim milk
1/4 cup Parmesan cheese

WHAT YOU NEED:

Cutting board
Sharp knife
Non-stick skillet
Baking sheet
Large spoon
Measuring cups
Oven mitts
Wire cooling rack

HOW YOU MAKE:

1. Preheat oven to 325 degrees Fahrenheit.

2. Chop onion, zucchini, and green pepper (see glossary).

3. In a non-stick skillet, cook fresh sliced mushrooms until their liquid is released but mushrooms are still firm (about 2 to 3 minutes).

4. Split each pita round to make 6 pizza servings and place on baking sheet.

5. Using large spoon spread pizza sauce evenly over the 6 rounds.

7. Top with mushrooms, onion, zucchini, green pepper, mozzarella cheese and Parmesan cheese.

8. Bake for 12 to 15 minutes. Remove from oven using oven mitts and cool on wire cooling rack.

Makes 6 servings.

NUTRIENT ANALYSIS PER SERVING:

Calories 195, carbohydrate 24g, protein 12g, fat 6g, saturated fat 3.5g, cholesterol 17mg, fiber 2g, sodium 369mg

FOOD EXCHANGES:
1 starch, 2 vegetables, 1/2 meat, 1/2 fat

Mmm-Mostaccioli

HOW YOU MAKE:

1. Mince garlic and onion (see glossary).

2. In a large skillet, cook ground meat over medium heat until well done, about 5 minutes, stirring occasionally with wooden spoon.

3. Spoon off excess fat using large spoon.

4. Add onion; cook until onion is golden, about 5 minutes. Do not let onion turn brown.

5. Add garlic, pepper, tomato sauce, tomato paste, basil and oregano.

6. Cover and simmer over low heat for about 25 minutes.

7. Meanwhile, cook noodles according to package directions omitting salt and oil.

8. Drain noodles with colander.

9. In a large bowl, toss noodles with tomato sauce. Serve immediately.

Makes 8 servings.

INGREDIENTS:

2 cloves garlic
1 large onion
3/4 pound ground sirloin tip
1/8 teaspoon pepper
1 can (22 ounces) tomato sauce
1 can (6 ounces) tomato paste
1/2 teaspoon basil
1/2 teaspoon oregano
3 cups uncooked mostaccioli

WHAT YOU NEED:

Cutting board
Sharp knife
Large skillet
Wooden spoon
Large saucepan
Colander
Large bowl

OCTOBER

NUTRIENT ANALYSIS PER SERVING:

Calories 288, carbohydrate 41g, protein 17g, fat 6.5g, saturated fat 2.5g, cholesterol 33mg, fiber 3.5g, sodium 672mg

FOOD EXCHANGES:
3 starch, 1 meat, 1 fat

NOVEMBER

Thanksgiving is a celebration of cooking, bringing all ages into the kitchen more than any other time. It's a time to share family traditions, stories and recipes.

The Yak loves to learn about the history of the holiday — and wants to share a recipe with you. Here's one for Corn Pudding that the early settlers may have shared at their table. The Yak's recipe is more modern to make it easier.

For a perfect drink for your Thanksgiving dinner, ladle out Cranberry Punch.

And here's a toast to say — or you can make up your own:

Here's to cooking together and eating together.

Photo by Kent Phillips

Tiny Corncakes

INGREDIENTS:

3/4 cup all-purpose flour
1/2 cup cornmeal
1 teaspoon baking powder
1/4 teaspoon salt
1/2 teaspoon sugar
1 can (14 3/4 ounces)
cream-style corn
1/2 cup skim milk
2 egg whites, slightly
beaten
Vegetable oil cooking spray

WHAT YOU NEED:

Large bowl
Large mixing spoon
Medium bowl
Griddle or large skillet
Pancake turner

HOW YOU MAKE:

1. In a large bowl, combine the flour, cornmeal, baking powder, salt and sugar. Stir well.

2. Make a well in center of mixture.

3. In a medium bowl, combine the cream-style corn, skim milk and egg whites. Add the milk mixture to the well in the flour mixture. Stir to combine, just until moistened.

4. Preheat a griddle or large skillet and spray with the vegetable oil cooking spray.

5. For each corncake, pour 3 tablespoons of the batter onto the hot griddle or skillet. Turn the corncakes when the tops are covered with bubbles and edges look cooked, and cook on the other side until done.

Makes 15 corncakes.

NUTRIENT ANALYSIS PER SERVING:

Calories 63, fat 0, saturated fat 0, cholesterol 0, protein 2g, sodium 157 mg, carbohydrate 14g, fiber 1g

FOOD EXCHANGES:
1 starch

Corn Pudding

HOW YOU MAKE:

1. Preheat oven to 350 degrees Fahrenheit.

2. Spray casserole dish with vegetable oil cooking spray.

3. Husk corn and remove the silk. Use a sharp knife and slice off the tops of the kernels into a bowl or drain canned corn and place in bowl. Add evaporated skim milk. Combine with remaining ingredients.

4. Pour into casserole dish. Place casserole dish in a pan of hot water. Bake until firm, about 45 minutes.

5. Remove from oven using oven mitts and cool about 15 minutes before serving.

Makes 8 servings.

Yak Fact · · · · · · · · · · · · · · ·

You need more than a balanced diet to be healthy. Exercise is also important. The key to a fit, trim body is simple. Balance the food you take in with the energy you use up. Almost any physical activity will burn up extra calories. Exercise is good for your heart, too.

INGREDIENTS:

Vegetable oil cooking spray
1 dozen ears fresh sweet corn (4 cups grated corn) or 4 cups canned corn (drained)
1 cup evaporated skim milk
2 eggs and 4 egg whites, lightly beaten
1 1/2 teaspoons salt
1/2 teaspoon pepper
2 tablespoons sugar
3 tablespoons melted tub margarine

WHAT YOU NEED:

Small sharp knife
Colander
Medium bowl
Rubber spatula
Measuring cups and spoons
1 1/2-quart casserole dish
Oven mitts

NUTRIENT ANALYSIS PER SERVING:

Calories 178, fat 6g, saturated fat 1g, cholesterol 54mg, protein 8g, sodium 504mg, carbohydrate 25g, fiber 2.5g

FOOD EXCHANGES:
1 1/2 starch, 1/2 meat, 1 fat

NOVEMBER

Glazed Carrots

INGREDIENTS:

6 medium carrots
2 teaspoons reduced-calorie, soft-tub, no trans-fats margarine
2 teaspoons brown sugar
1/2 teaspoon fresh minced ginger root or dash of ground ginger

WHAT YOU NEED:

Vegetable peeler
Cutting board
Sharp knife
2-quart saucepan
Small saucepan
Wooden spoon
Measuring spoons

HOW YOU MAKE:

1. Scrape carrots with a vegetable peeler and cut on a cutting board with a sharp knife into julienne strips about four inches long and 1/4-inch wide (see glossary).

2. Heat one inch of water to boiling in a 2-quart saucepan.

3. Add carrots.

4. Heat to boiling; reduce heat to low. Boil gently for 18 to 20 minutes until carrots are tender (poke with a fork).

5. Meanwhile, melt margarine in a small saucepan; stir in brown sugar and ginger and cook over medium heat, stirring constantly, until sugar dissolves, about 5 minutes.

6. Add carrots and stir gently, until well coated.

Makes 6 servings.

Yak Fact

An easy way to reduce saturated fat and lower cholesterol is to use tub margarine in place of butter. Look for the margarines that say "no trans-fats" on the label.

NUTRIENT ANALYSIS PER CUP:

Calories 36, carbohydrate 7g, protein 1g, fat 1g, saturated fat 0, cholesterol 0, fiber 2g, sodium 37mg

FOOD EXCHANGES:
1 vegetable, 1/2 fat

NOVEMBER

Cranberry Punch

HOW YOU MAKE:

1. Mix cranberry juice and lemon-lime soda in punch bowl.

2. Serve.

Makes 14 one-cup servings.

INGREDIENTS:

1 1/2 quarts cranberry juice
2 quarts lemon-lime
soda pop

WHAT YOU NEED:

Punch bowl
Ladle

Yak Fact • • • •

Water is critical to life. Your body is more than half water. To stay healthy, you need to drink plenty of water, juices and other beverages. When you work out, keep a water bottle handy. That way your body won't become dehydrated (lose too much water).

NUTRIENT ANALYSIS PER CUP:

Calories 118, carbohydrate 30g, protein 0, fat 0, saturated fat 0, cholesterol 0, fiber 0, sodium 18mg

FOOD EXCHANGES:
2 fruit

Turkey Tacos

INGREDIENTS:

1 hot chili pepper
2 garlic cloves
1 medium onion
1 large tomato
1 pound turkey breast, cooked
2 teaspoons canola oil
1/2 teaspoon ground cumin
1/4 teaspoon dried cilantro
3 tablespoons low-sodium tomato paste
3/4 cup water
2 tablespoons lime juice
8 flour tortillas
4 ounces skim milk mozzarella cheese, shredded
1 1/2 cup shredded lettuce

WHAT YOU NEED:

Cutting board
Chef's knife
Non-stick skillet with top
Wooden spoon
Microwave
Measuring cups
Measuring spoons
Wax paper

HOW YOU MAKE:

1. Mince chili pepper and garlic (see glossary).

2. Chop onion and tomato (see glossary).

3. Cut turkey into chunks or shred.

4. In a non-stick skillet, heat oil and saute hot chili pepper, onion and garlic until tender.

5. Add turkey to skillet. Season with cumin, oregano, cilantro and mix well with wooden spoon.

6. Add tomato paste, water and lime juice. Mix well.

7. Bring mixture to a boil. Cover and simmer 5 minutes or until liquid is absorbed.

8. Warm tortillas in a hot cast iron skillet for one minute on each side, or stack alternately with wax paper, place in a microwave, and heat for 20-30 seconds on 100 percent (high) power.

9. Top each tortilla with equal amounts of turkey mixture, cheese, lettuce and tomato.

10. Fold each tortilla in half to form tacos.

Makes 8 tacos.

NOVEMBER

NUTRIENT ANALYSIS PER TACO:

Calories 236, carbohydrate 23g, protein 22g, fat 6g, saturated fat 2.5g, cholesterol 49mg, fiber 2g, sodium 253mg

FOOD EXCHANGES:

1 starch, 1 vegetable, 2 1/2 meat

Harvest Potluck Casserole

HOW YOU MAKE:

1. Wash sweet potatoes.

2. In a large saucepan, place sweet potatoes and cover with water. Bring to boil and boil potatoes nearly tender (about 10 minutes).

3. Drain, cool, peel and slice sweet potatoes.

4. While the sweet potatoes are cooking, wash, core and slice the apples (see glossary).

5. Preheat oven to 350 degrees Fahrenheit.

6. Spray 3-quart baking dish with vegetable oil cooking spray.

7. Place half of the sliced sweet potatoes in baking dish. Cover with half of the apples.

8. Drizzle on 1 teaspoon lemon juice.

9. Sprinkle with half the brown sugar and cinnamon. Dot with half of the margarine.

10. Repeat to make another layer with remaining 1 teaspoon lemon juice and 1 tablespoon margarine.

11. Bake 45 minutes or until top is brown.

12. Using oven mitts, remove pan from oven.

Makes 6 servings.

INGREDIENTS:

3 to 4 medium sweet potatoes
2 medium tart apples
Vegetable oil cooking spray
2 teaspoons fresh lemon juice, divided
2/3 cup dark brown sugar
1 teaspoon ground cinnamon
2 tablespoons frozen tub margarine, no-trans fat, divided

WHAT YOU NEED:

Large saucepan with top
Cutting board
Chef's knife
3-quart baking dish
Measuring cups
Measuring spoons
Oven mitts

NUTRIENT ANALYSIS PER SERVING:

Calories 215, carbohydrate 45g, protein 2g, fat 4g, saturated fat 1g, cholesterol 0, fiber 3g, sodium 69mg

FOOD EXCHANGES:
3 starch, 1 fat

NOVEMBER

Best Birthday Cake

INGREDIENTS:

Cake:
1 1/4 cup sugar, divided
1/2 cup cocoa
1 cup buttermilk, divided
1/2 cup soft tub margarine
4 egg whites
2 cups cake flour
1 teaspoon baking soda
1/8 teaspoon salt
1 teaspoon vanilla
Vegetable oil cooking spray

Frosting:
2 tablespoons margarine
4 tablespoons cocoa
1 cup sifted powdered sugar
1/2 teaspoon vanilla
2 tablespoons skim milk

WHAT YOU NEED:

Hand mixer
Medium bowl
Rubber spatula
Large bowl
Sifter
Tube pan
Wire rack
Small bowl
Measuring cups
Measuring spoons
Oven mitts
Wax paper

HOW YOU MAKE:

1. Preheat oven to 350 degrees Fahrenheit.

2. In a medium bowl, using hand mixer, beat 3/4 cup sugar, cocoa and 1/2 cup buttermilk until well blended. Clean sides with rubber spatula.

3. In a large bowl, beat margarine with rubber spatula until soft, gradually adding the remaining 1/2 cup sugar.

4. Add egg whites and beat until blended.

5. Beat in cocoa mixture.

6. Sift cake flour onto wax paper. Resift with baking soda and salt.

7. Add the flour in three parts to the margarine mixture, alternately with remaining 1/2 cup buttermilk and vanilla. Beat batter after each addition until smooth.

Yak Fact · · · ·

Although your body can tell you when to eat, it can't tell you what to eat. Candy and soda pop might fill you up but they won't give your body what it needs to work well.

8. Spray tube pan with vegetable oil cooking spray and flour well.

9. Pour cake batter into pan and bake about one hour.

10. Using oven mitts, remove cake from oven. Let cake cool 10 minutes and then remove from pan and finish cooling on wire rack.

11. In a small bowl, using a hand mixer, combine margarine and cocoa. Beat at medium speed until smooth.

12. Add powdered sugar and vanilla. Mix well. Scrape sides of bowl with rubber spatula.

13. Gradually add milk, 1 teaspoon at a time, and beat until smooth.

14. Spread mixture over top of cake

Makes 16 slices.

NUTRIENT ANALYSIS PER SLICE:

Calories 213, carbohydrate 34g, protein 3g, fat 7g, saturated fat 1.5g, cholesterol 1mg, fiber 0.5g, sodium 231mg

FOOD EXCHANGES:
2 starch, 1 1/2 fat

NOVEMBER

DECEMBER

December brings short days, long nights and lots of time to spend in the kitchen baking goodies for family and friends. It's often a busy time, though, with school events and holiday shopping, so help mom and dad out. A casserole is as fun to make as a family as it is to eat together.

There are lots of celebrations in this month: Hanukkah, Christmas and Kwanzaa, to name a few. All the holidays include celebrating with food.

It's a fun and festive time — ending with New Year's Eve, the final food celebration of the year.

Sugar cookies are sure to please everyone all month long. Check out our basic recipe (you can keep the dough ready in the freezer for whenever you have the time).

And what goes with cookies? Hot chocolate. While you're in the kitchen decorating cookies, treat yourself to a yummy mug of hot chocolate — with peppermint sticks to stir it. Happy cooking and Happy New Year!

Photo by Kent Phillips

Tasty Tuna Casserole

INGREDIENTS:

1/2 medium onion
8 ounces uncooked macaroni
Vegetable oil cooking spray
1 can (10 3/4 ounces) low-fat, reduced sodium, condensed cream of mushroom soup
1/8 teaspoon pepper
1 can (about 6 ounces) water-packed tuna, drained
1 package (10 1/2 ounces) frozen mixed vegetables (thawed)
1 tablespoon Parmesan cheese
1 tablespoon unseasoned bread crumbs

WHAT YOU NEED:

Cutting board
Sharp knife
Large saucepan
Wooden spoon
Colander
2-quart casserole dish
Measuring spoons
Rubber spatula
Large bowl
Oven mitts
Small bowl
Spoon

HOW YOU MAKE:

1. Chop onion (see glossary).

2. Preheat oven to 350 degrees Fahrenheit.

3. Cook macaroni as directed on package, omitting salt. Drain in colander and set aside.

4. Spray a 2-quart casserole dish with the vegetable oil cooking spray and set aside.

5. In a large bowl, combine cream of mushroom soup, onion, pepper, frozen mixed vegetables and tuna. Mix well.

6. Stir in cooked macaroni.

7. Using rubber spatula, pour mixture into the prepared casserole dish.

8. In a small bowl, using a spoon combine the Parmesan cheese and bread crumbs. Sprinkle the top of the tuna mixture with the cheese mixture.

10. Bake for 30-35 minutes or until the sauce is bubbly and crumb topping is golden.

11. Using oven mitts remove from the oven and serve.

Makes 4 servings.

NUTRIENT ANALYSIS PER SERVING:

Calories 369, carbohydrate 61g, protein 22g, fat 3.5g, saturated fat 1g, cholesterol 27mg, fiber 4.5g, sodium 390mg

FOOD EXCHANGES:
3 1/2 starch,
2 vegetable, 1 meat

Super Spaghetti Casserole

HOW YOU MAKE:

1. Chop onion (see glossary).

2. Julienne green pepper (see glossary).

3. Preheat oven to 350 degrees Fahrenheit.

4. Spray a 9-inch by 13-inch baking pan with vegetable oil cooking spray. Set aside.

5. Cook the spaghetti according to package directions omitting the salt and oil.

6. Use a colander to rinse and drain.

7. With a large spoon, combine the cooked spaghetti, Parmesan cheese, margarine and egg substitute in the prepared pan. Set aside.

8. Spray a non-stick skillet with vegetable oil cooking spray. Add the ground turkey and brown over medium heat along with the chopped onion, mixing with wooden spoon.

9. Spoon the turkey mixture over the noodles. Pour the spaghetti sauce over all.

10. Sprinkle with mozzarella cheese. Arrange green pepper strips over the top.

11. Cover with aluminum foil and bake for 20 minutes or until the cheese melts and the mixture is bubbling.

12. Using oven mitts, remove and let stand 5-10 minutes before cutting.

Makes 8 servings.

INGREDIENTS:

1 small onion
1 green bell pepper
Vegetable oil cooking spray
1 pound spaghetti noodles
1/3 cup fat-free Parmesan cheese
2 tablespoons fat-free margarine
1/2 cup fat-free egg substitute
1 pound ground turkey breast
1 jar (26 ounces) low-fat spaghetti sauce
1 cup (4 ounces) part-skim mozzarella cheese

WHAT YOU NEED:

Cutting board
Chef's knife
9-inch x 13-inch baking pan
Large saucepan
Colander
Large spoon
Non-stick skillet
Wooden spoon
Aluminum foil
Oven mitts
Measuring cups
Measuring spoons

NUTRIENT ANALYSIS PER SERVING:

Calories 372, carbohydrate 54g, protein 29g, fat 4g, saturated fat 1.5g, cholesterol 49mg, fiber 3.5g, sodium 430mg

FOOD EXCHANGES:
3 starch, 1 vegetable, 2 1/2 lean meat

Peanut Butter Crispy Marshmallow Bars

INGREDIENTS:

Vegetable oil cooking spray
10 ounces miniature marshmallows
2 tablespoons canola oil
1 teaspoon vanilla
1/2 cup peanut butter
6 cups crisp rice cereal

WHAT YOU NEED:

9-inch by-13-inch baking pan
Large microwave-safe bowl
Measuring cups
Measuring spoons
Spatula

HOW YOU MAKE:

1. Spray a 9-inch by 13-inch pan with the vegetable oil cooking spray.

2. Place the marshmallows in a large microwave-safe bowl.

3. Sprinkle the marshmallows with canola oil and vanilla. Toss to coat so each of the marshmallows is coated with oil.

4. Add in the peanut butter.

5. Microwave on high for 1 1/2 to 2 minutes or until the marshmallows are melted, stirring once. Stir until smooth.

6. Stir the cereal into the marshmallow mixture. Stir until equally combined.

7. Press the mixture into the prepared pan as evenly as possible (if the mixture is sticking to hands, press with wax paper sprayed with cooking spray).

8. Cool. Then cut into bars.

Makes 18 bars.

 Yak Fact • • • • • • • • • • • • • •

Good types of fat, such as the monounsaturated fats found in canola and olive oil, will keep your heart healthy.

NUTRIENT ANALYSIS PER SERVING:

Calories 138, carbohydrate 22g, protein 3g, fat 5g, saturated fat 1g, cholesterol 0mg, fiber 0.5g, sodium 102mg

FOOD EXCHANGES:
1 1/2 starch, 1 fat

DECEMBER

Potato Latkes

HOW YOU MAKE:

1. Grate the potatoes. On a cutting board, using a sharp knife, chop onion (see glossary).

2. In a large bowl, mix potatoes and onion. Stir in egg whites and mix well.

3. Add bread crumbs, pepper and salt to make a loose but not watery mixture.

4. Pre-heat oven to 350 degrees Fahrenheit.

5. Heat vegetable oil in a large non-stick skillet over medium heat.

6. To make each pancake, drop about 1/4 cup of the potato mixture into the skillet and flatten into a rounded rectangle about two inches by three inches, just under 1/4-inch thick. Lightly brown pancakes on one side, turn and brown on the other side. Make sure they are cooked enough on one side before flipping or they will fall apart.

7. Transfer the pancakes to a baking sheet that has been lightly coated with vegetable oil cooking spray, stacking pancakes on top of each other.

8. Bake pancakes about 15 minutes. Turn once and bake another 10 minutes.

9. Transfer to a platter and blot with paper towels before serving.

Makes 24 pancakes.

INGREDIENTS:

6 medium potatoes
1 onion
2 egg whites
1/4 cup bread crumbs
Black pepper to taste
1/2 teaspoon salt
2 tablespoons canola oil
Vegetable oil cooking spray

WHAT YOU NEED:

Grater
Cutting board
Sharp knife
Large bowl
Large non-stick skillet
Measuring cups
Measuring spoons
Baking sheet
Platter
Paper towels

NUTRIENT ANALYSIS PER PANCAKE:

Calories 41, carbohydrate 7g, protein 1g, fat 1g, saturated fat 0, cholesterol 0mg, fiber 0.5g, sodium 64 mg

FOOD EXCHANGES:
1/2 starch, 1/2 fat

DECEMBER

Super Sugar Cookies

INGREDIENTS:

3/4 cup sugar
1/3 cup tub margarine
2 egg whites
1 teaspoon vanilla
1/3 cup vanilla non-fat yogurt
3 cups all-purpose flour, divided
1 teaspoon baking powder
1/2 teaspoon baking soda
1/4 teaspoon ground nutmeg
Vegetable oil cooking spray
Colored sprinkles, optional

WHAT YOU NEED:

Hand mixer
Medium bowl
Rubber spatula
Large bowl
2 baking sheets
Rolling pin
2-inch cookie cutter
Wire rack
Oven mitts
Measuring cups
Measuring spoons

HOW YOU MAKE:

1. In a medium bowl, cream the sugar and margarine until fluffy, about 2 to 3 minutes.

2. Add the egg whites one at a time, beating after each addition.

3. Add the vanilla and yogurt and mix well. Scrape sides of bowl with rubber spatula.

4. In a large bowl, sift together 2 2/3 cup flour, baking powder, baking soda and nutmeg. Add gradually to yogurt mixture. Mix well.

5. Divide the dough into 3 equal parts and press into disc shapes. Cover and chill for at least 3 hours.

6. At baking time, preheat oven to 425 degrees Fahrenheit.

7. Spray two baking sheets with vegetable oil cooking spray.

8. Sprinkle the remaining 1/3 cup flour on the work surface.

9. Roll each part of the cookie dough to 1/4-inch thick on the floured surface.

10. Cut with 2-inch cookie cutter.

11. Place cookies on the prepared baking sheets. If desired, decorate with sprinkles.

12. Bake until no indentation remains when touched, about 6 to 8 minutes.

13. Using oven mitts, remove from the oven and place cookies on a wire rack to cool.

Makes 48 cookies.

NUTRIENT ANALYSIS PER COOKIE:

Calories 54, carbohydrate 9g, protein 1g, fat 1g, saturated fat 0, cholesterol 0, fiber 0, sodium 41mg

FOOD EXCHANGES:
3/4 starch

DECEMBER

Creamy Hot Chocolate

HOW YOU MAKE:

1. Mix cocoa and sugar in a saucepan.

2. Stir in water and heat over medium heat, stirring constantly, until mixture is smooth.

3. Heat to boiling, reduce heat to low. Simmer uncovered 4 minutes, stirring constantly.

4. Stir in milk and vanilla. Heat just until hot (do not boil).

5. Beat with hand beater until foamy, or stir until smooth. Divide up into 6 mugs and add peppermint stick to each if desired. Serve immediately.

Makes six 1-cup servings.

INGREDIENTS:

1/3 cup baking cocoa
1/3 cup sugar
1 1/2 cups water
4 1/2 cups skim milk
1/2 teaspoon vanilla
6 peppermint sticks (optional)

WHAT YOU NEED:

1 1/2 quart saucepan
Measuring cups
Measuring spoons
Mixing spoon
Hand beater
Mugs

NUTRIENT ANALYSIS PER 1-CUP SERVING:

(does not include peppermint stick)
Calories 124, carbohydrate 22g, protein 7g, fat 1g, saturated fat 0.5g, cholesterol 3mg, fiber 1g, sodium 97mg

FOOD EXCHANGES:
1 milk, 1/2 starch

DECEMBER

Veggie Pizza Treats

INGREDIENTS:

2 green onions
1 cup broccoli florets
1 small sweet red pepper
1 cup cauliflower florets
1/2 cup sliced mushrooms
12 ounces fat-free block
cream cheese, softened
2 ounces (1/2 cup) fat-free
shredded cheddar cheese
1 package (10 ounce)
refrigerated pizza dough

WHAT YOU NEED:

Cutting board
Sharp knife
Baking sheet
Measuring cups or
kitchen scale
Oven mitts
Cooling rack

HOW YOU MAKE:

1. Chop green onion, broccoli, red pepper and cauliflower (see glossary).

2. Place the pizza dough on a baking sheet and press into a 9-inch by 13-inch rectangle.

3. Bake according to package directions.

4. Remove from oven using oven mitts. Place on cooling rack.

5. While dough is still warm, spread cream cheese evenly over the dough.

6. Sprinkle evenly with green onion, broccoli, red pepper, mushrooms, cauliflower and shredded cheese.

7. Chill in the refrigerator until serving time.

Makes 8 pieces.

Yak Fact • • • • • • • • • • • • • • • • • •

A calorie measures the amount of energy stored in food.

NUTRIENT ANALYSIS PER PIECE:

Calories 155, carbohydrate 23g, protein 12g, fat 2g, saturated fat 0.5g, cholesterol 3mg, fiber 1.5g, sodium 512mg

FOOD EXCHANGES:
1 bread, 1 vegetable, 1 meat

DECEMBER

Spicy Chicken Nuggets

HOW YOU MAKE:

1. Preheat oven to 450 degrees Fahrenheit.

2. Line baking sheet with aluminum foil and lightly spray with vegetable oil cooking spray.

3. Place cornflakes in a heavy duty zippered-lock plastic bag. Crush cereal by using a rolling pin or meat mallet.

4. In a medium bowl, place cornflakes, Parmesan cheese and Cajun seasoning; mix with large spoon.

5. Place egg substitute in a small bowl.

6. On a cutting board, using a sharp knife, cut chicken breasts into 24 chunks.

7. Dip each chicken chunk into the egg substitute and then roll it in the crumb mixture until it is coated on all sides. Repeat with all chunks.

8. Place chicken on prepared baking sheet. Bake for 4 to 5 minutes, remove from oven using oven mitts and flip the nuggets over with pancake turner; return to oven for another 4 to 5 minutes until chicken is medium golden brown and cooked throughout. Remove from oven with mitts and set on wire cooling rack.

9. To make dip for chicken nuggets, mix together the mustard, mayonnaise and honey in a small bowl until smooth. Serve with chicken nuggets.

Makes 6 servings.

Cook's Note: Children under the age of 1 should not eat honey.

INGREDIENTS:

Vegetable oil cooking spray
1 1/2 cups cornflakes
1/2 cup grated fat-free Parmesan cheese
1 1/2 teaspoons Cajun seasonings
1/2 cup fat-free egg substitute
1 1/2 pounds boneless, skinless chicken breasts
1/2 cup Dijon mustard
1/4 cup low-fat mayonnaise or salad dressing
2 tablespoons honey

WHAT YOU NEED:

Baking sheet
Aluminum foil
Heavy duty zippered-lock plastic bag
Rolling pin or meat mallet
Medium bowl, 2 small bowls
Large spoon
Cutting board
Sharp knife
Measuring cups
Measuring spoons
Pancake turner

NUTRIENT ANALYSIS PER SERVING:

Calories 283, carbohydrate 18g, protein 35, fat 7g, saturated fat 1.5g, cholesterol 87mg, fiber 0.5g, sodium 437mg

FOOD EXCHANGES:
1 starch, 4 1/2 lean meat

DECEMBER

Winning recipes from you!

Yak's Corner kids are creative cooks. We couldn't pick just one recipe from the many you shared in our Yak's Corner-Heart Smart® cookbook contest. We did find that many of you enjoy time in the kitchen with your family. Our first recipe is from the brother and sister team of Veronica and Evan Allen. They say their Dad loves this salad. Sounds like a good choice for Father's Day — or anytime dad needs a treat.

PHOTO BY RICHARD LEE

Dad's Boffo Bean Salad

HOW YOU MAKE:

1. On cutting board, peel and chop onion, reserving a few nice rings for decoration (see glossary).

2. Drain and rinse the beans.

3. Combine green beans, wax beans, kidney beans, garbanzo beans, chopped onion, sugar, canola oil and white vinegar in a large glass or plastic bowl.

4. Top with reserved onion rings.

Cook's Notes:

✪ For best results, make the day before. Refrigerate and retoss two or three times before serving.

✪ Decreasing the canola oil from 1/2 cup to 1/4 cup will decrease the total calories in this salad to 100 and the total fat to 4 grams, per serving.

Makes 16 servings.

Prepared by Evan and Veronica Allen of Livonia, Michigan.

INGREDIENTS:

1 can green beans
1 can wax beans
1 can kidney beans
1 can garbanzo beans
1 medium yellow onion
1/2 cup granulated sugar
1/2 cup canola oil
1/2 cup white vinegar

WHAT YOU NEED:

Cutting board
Chef's knife
Can opener
Colander
Large glass or plastic bowl
Large mixing spoon
Measuring cups
Mixing spoons

NUTRIENT ANALYSIS PER SERVING:

Calories 129, carbohydrate 15g, protein 3g, fat 7g, saturated fat 0.5g, cholesterol 0, fiber 2.5g, sodium 227mg

FOOD EXCHANGES:
1 starch, 1 1/2 fat

Winning recipes from you!

This recipe comes from Bianca Valverde of Ecorse. Bianca just can't get enough of guacamole! We bet you'll like this, too. Does it look like green slime? That's just a fun name, but it's sure a tasty treat. Thanks, Bianca, for sharing with the Yak!

PHOTO BY RICHARD LEE

Slime Guacamole

HOW YOU MAKE:

1. Cut avocados in half and remove pits.

2. On a cutting board, chop tomato and onion (see glossary).

3. Smash avocados in a bowl.

4. Pour lemon juice into avocados one teaspoon at a time, mixing thoroughly after each addition.

5. Mix in chopped tomato and onion.

6. Serve with baked tortilla chips.

Makes 2 cups.

Prepared by Bianca Valverde of Ecorse.

INGREDIENTS:

2 ripe avocados
4 teaspoons of lemon juice
1 large ripe tomato
1 teaspoon chopped onion
1 pound baked tortilla chips

WHAT YOU NEED:

Cutting board
Chef's knife
Medium bowl
Rubber spatula
Measuring spoons
Mixing spoon

NUTRIENT ANALYSIS PER 2 TABLESPOONS SAUCE, 1 OUNCE BAKED TORTILLA CHIPS:

Calories 155, carbohydrate 28g, protein 3g, fat 4g, saturated fat 0.5g, cholesterol 0, fiber 4g, sodium 203mg

FOOD EXCHANGES:
1/2 starch, 1 vegetable, 1/2 fat

Now you're cooking!

You've now read lots of good recipes in this cookbook. But you can't just serve a dessert — or drink — by itself. What are you going to serve for the main course?

That's where meal planning comes in. Before you start preparing a meal, think about all the pieces coming together — for example, a drink, main course, side dishes and dessert. (The food pyramid on page 136 is a good guide to help you figure how many servings of different foods your body needs every day.)

You also want your plate to look good. One trick is to make sure you use an assortment of colors in the food you serve. For example, a fruit salad not only offers you a healthy variety of vitamins, it also is a colorful addition to your table.

You'll want to think about contrasts in flavors and texture of food, too. A spicy Mexican dish calls out for a refreshing cool drink. A soup calls out for something crunchy on the side, like a crusty roll, and some carrots and celery sticks.

It's really simple. Think about what you like and plan a meal that's healthy — but also fun. We organized this cookbook by

PHOTO BY KENT PHILLIPS

month, giving you ideas for timely meals to fit the season. But don't be afraid to mix and match recipes from every season. Here are some menu ideas to get you started. You can experiment and adapt them to your family's liking. Get cooking.

Make a Meal

✪ indicates this recipe is in our cookbook

BREAKFAST
✪ Fabulous French Toast
Sliced Melon
✪ Creamy Hot Chocolate

✪ Made for Mom
Breakfast Pie
Sliced Fruit
Whole Wheat Toast
Skim Milk and/or Orange
Juice

✪ Blueberry Pancakes with
✪ Blueberry Sauce
1/2 Pink Grapefruit
Skim Milk

LUNCH
✪ Sunday Salad
Whole Wheat Pita
Carrot Sticks
Skim Milk

✪ Hot Tuna Pockets
Pretzels
Apple Slices
✪ Chocolate Brownie Heart

✪ Pleasing Pita Pockets
✪ Microwaved Cinnamon
Spiced Applesauce
✪ Backpack Granola Bars
Orange Juice

DINNER
✪ Super Spaghetti
Casserole
✪ Zesty French Bread
Tossed Salad with Low-Fat
Salad Dressing
Skim Milk

✪ Tasty Tuna Casserole
Fruit Cocktail in Light Syrup
Bread Sticks
Skim Milk

Roasted Turkey Breast
✪ Harvest Potluck
Casserole
Green Beans
Whole Wheat Dinner Rolls
Skim Milk

✪ Oven-Fried Chicken
Baked Potato with Low-Fat
or Fat-Free Sour Cream
✪ Brain-Boosting Salad
Skim Milk

✪ Spicy Chicken Nuggets
✪ Rice Pilaf
Broccoli Trees
Tossed Salad with Low-
Fat Salad Dressing
Skim Milk

SPECIAL DAYS
Father's Day
✪ Dad's Sloppy Joes
✪ Oven-Baked French Fries
✪ Corn on the Cob
✪ Strawberry Shortcake

Sleepover Party
✪ Pita Pizza Treats
✪ Marshmallow Fruit Dip
✪ S'more Snack Cake
✪ Very Beary Snack Mix

Halloween Party
✪ Spicy Warm Cider
✪ Pumpkin Cookie Sticks
✪ Veggie Pizza Treats
✪ Candy Corn Cupcakes

4th of July Party
✪ Stuffed Burger
✪ Deluxe Coleslaw
Raw vegetable sticks
✪ 4th of July Parfait

Super Bowl Party
✪ Super Bowl Subs
Raw vegetable sticks
✪ Chocolate Oatmeal
Treats

Making Meals Special

Now you're cooking. You have recipes and know your way around the kitchen — but you have to bring it all together on the table. Don't think of setting the table as a chore. After all, your great cooking deserves to be treated like a work of art! Here are some rules for setting a table — and ideas to inspire you to make every meal a special celebration.

It's not over once you know where to place the knife and fork. How about a centerpiece? A bowl of fruit, candles — or even your main dish — can give your table a pretty focus. For some holidays, you can add more decorations. Stick small flags into a loaf of bread or into muffins for the Fourth of July.

PHOTO BY KENT PHILLIPS

Setting the table correctly means putting the fork to the left and the knife and spoon to the right, as shown. This photo shows a setting for a simple meal.

For New Year's Eve, decorate the table with party horns and noisemakers.

You can add all kinds of special touches to each person's place, too. For a big gathering or more formal table, make name cards on colorful construction paper.

Another way to dress up the table is with napkins. Paper napkins, which come with all kinds of patterns, are inexpensive and easy to find. Or you can try cloth napkins — and dress them up even more by adding napkin rings. If you don't have napkin rings, simply tie ribbon around cloth or paper napkins. (Think about gold and silver ribbon for New Year's or school colors for a football Saturday.)

You can even make your own place mats. Use sheets of big construction paper. Think about creating artwork tied to a theme (like hearts for Valentine's Day on red construction paper). You'll want to have your parents get your placemats laminated before using.

PHOTO BY KENT PHILLIPS

This place setting breaks the rules — with a triangle design. Try a creative setting, too!

Good Sports!

Kirk Maltby

Ron Rice

Aaron Ward

Ask an athlete if you want to get some great tips on good eating. These athletes shared some of their favorite power boosters in the fruit and vegetable group.

FROM THE DETROIT RED WINGS:

Pat Verbeek: Broccoli and plums.
Kirk Maltby: Corn on the cob and Granny Smith apples.
Aaron Ward: Green beans and bananas.

PHOTO BY PATRICIA BECK

FROM THE DETROIT LIONS:

Luther Elliss: Strawberries and kiwis.
Tracy Scroggins: Oranges and spinach.
Ron Rice: Grapes and kiwi.
Ray Roberts: Bananas, pineapples and spinach.

Good Sports!

And what about milk? The Got Milk campaign and popular photos of milk-mustached athletes have given milk a boost. Athletes who swear by milk-power include tennis stars Serena and Venus Williams and soccer champ Mia Hamm. Check out **www.whymilk.com** for why milk has some mooovers and shakers.

PHOTO BY MARY SCHROEDER

PHOTO BY J. KYLE KEENER

Mia Hamm

Serena Williams

Venus Williams

Just for parents!

Here are 10 Ways to Raise a Heart Smart Child:

1. Set a good example. Don't expect your children to eat their vegetables and drink their milk if you are drinking soda pop and avoiding vegetables at the same meal.

2. Offer a variety of healthful, great-tasting foods to your children at regularly scheduled times. Research shows that the more often children are exposed to a certain food, the more likely they are to like it. Sometimes it takes up to 10 tries before a child will decide s/he likes broccoli. So don't give up.

3. Let your children decide how much of that food they are going to eat. Young children know when they are hungry and when they are not. No amount of cajoling

on the parents part is going to get a toddler to eat when he/she doesn't want to. And forcing older children to clean their plates only encourages overeating later in life.

4. Avoid calling foods good and bad. All foods can fit into a Heart Smart diet. Instead teach your children that some foods are OK occasionally while others can be enjoyed every day.

5. Eat as many meals as possible together, as a family. Research published in 2000 found that children ages 9 to 14 who eat a family dinner are more likely than their peers to consume fruits and vegetable and less likely to drink soda or eat high-fat or sugar-laden foods. This led to higher intakes of fiber and may nutrients, including calcium, folate, vitamins B_6, B_{12}, C and E and iron.

6. Don't bribe your children with food. Threatening that there will

be no dessert if they don't eat their vegetables only teaches children to value dessert. It doesn't teach them to like vegetables.

7. Similarly, don't use food as a reward. Verbal praise, hugs and kisses for good behavior go much further in reinforcing good deeds than a slice of cake or a bowl of ice cream.

8. Allow your children to pick the vegetable that is going to be served at a meal. Don't ask them if they want vegetables, but give them a choice: would you like carrots or green beans with dinner tonight? Teach your children that fruits and vegetables are a part of every meal, but there are many options, and let him/her make that choice.

9. Avoid talking in front of your children about dieting, counting calories and/or feeling fat.

10. And finally, teach your children how to cook. Use this cookbook to help

Just for parents!

him/her learn how to plan nutritious meals and prepare them. Teach him/her that preparing healthy meals and snacks can be tasty and fun. Not only is this an important life skill, you will get a chance to spend some quality time together.

You can use this book with children of all ages, from two-year-olds all the way through adolescents. Explain the rules of the kitchen to your children. Is it okay for them to use any of the appliances without your supervision? How about knives? Let them know up front what you are comfortable with them doing on their own, and when they should ask for adult help. The more experience they get, the sooner you will feel comfortable letting them loose in the kitchen. Before you know it, they may want to take a turn preparing an entire meal, on their own! Here are some general guidelines to help you decide what your rules will be:

2-6 YEAR-OLDS:

At this age kids can help dump ingredients into a mixing bowl, help stir foods and learn about kitchen safety. They also would enjoy choosing some of the items that will be served from a short list of options.

6-8 YEAR-OLDS:

This age group can measure out the food using measuring cups and spoons.

8-12 YEAR-OLDS:

Kids are eager to help in the kitchen. There's a huge sense of accomplishment in meal preparation. You can trust them to read recipes, measure and even handle basic appliances like the microwave and toaster oven. Parents should be on hand to help with using the oven and slicing and dicing.

12-18 YEAR-OLDS:

With a few lessons on safety from you, at this age most children can operate most kitchen appliances and use sharp knives for cutting and chopping.

Pyramid Power

The Food Pyramid is a graphic to help children and adults better understand balanced eating and what and how much to eat from each food group. Servings are kid-sized. You can download your own copy of the new pyramid on the Internet at

www.usda.gov/news/usdakids/index.html

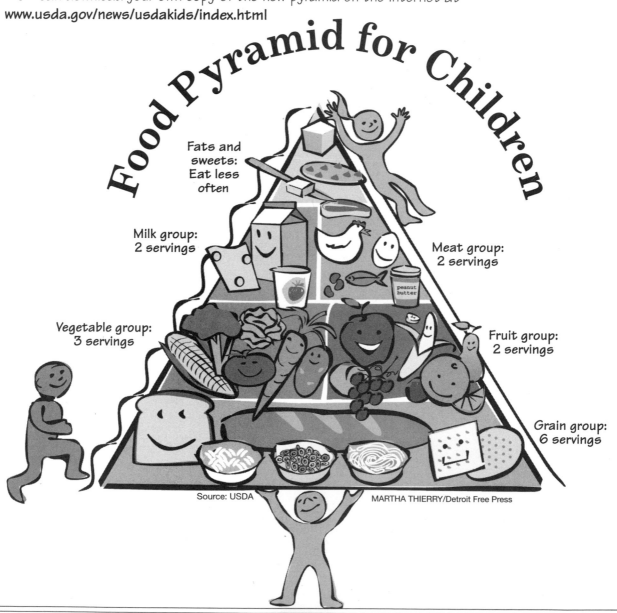

Food Pyramid for Children

Fats and sweets: Eat less often

Milk group: 2 servings

Meat group: 2 servings

Vegetable group: 3 servings

Fruit group: 2 servings

Grain group: 6 servings

peanut butter

Source: USDA   MARTHA THIERRY/Detroit Free Press

Portion Sizes

1 SERVING OF FRUITS OR VEGETABLES = TENNIS BALL

1 SERVING OF BREAD = CASSETTE TAPE

1 MEDIUM POTATO = COMPUTER MOUSE

1 OUNCE MEATBALL = GOLF BALL
(SERVING SIZE IS 3 OUNCES, THEREFORE 3 GOLF BALLS)

3 OUNCES MEAT (1 SERVING) = DECK OF CARDS

1 SERVING OF CHEESE = 2 DOMINOES

1 SERVING PASTA, RICE, HOT CEREAL = HOCKEY PUCK

1 SERVING COLD CEREAL = BASEBALL

Good Eating, Good Exercise

PHOTO BY MARY SCHROEDER

Metabolism (meh-TAB-uh-liz-um): The way your body converts the foods you eat to energy. Exercise increases what is called your metabolic rate so that your body burns more calories to fuel your active muscles.

Fitness: The measure of a healthy body. It's lifelong. The three most common measures of fitness are how strong your muscles are, how long you can keep going during exercise and how easily you can bend and move.

Calorie: A calorie is a measure of how much energy is in a food. When the number of calories you eat is the same as the number of calories your body burns, your weight remains the same.

Aerobic (uh-ro-bick) exercise: Any activity that uses lots of oxygen and causes your breathing and heart rate to increase — preferably for at least 15 or 20 minutes. It's not the type of exercise but how you do it: steadily, with no rests. Aerobic exercise strengthens your heart and lungs, burns body fat and gives you endurance.

Fitness Power

Physical Activity Pyramid

LEVEL 4

Not too often:
Inactivity –
watching TV
and sitting

LEVEL 3

2-3 times
per week:
Flexibility
exercises –
stretching

2-3 times per week:
Muscle fitness
exercises –
weight training
and calisthenics

LEVEL 2

3-5 times per week:
Active aerobics –
biking, swimming,
and jogging

3-5 times per week:
Recreational
hobbies and sports –
tennis, basketball,
dancing,
martial arts,
baseball,
soccer

LEVEL 1

Everyday
activity –   walk to school,
climb the stairs,
play in the park,
in-line skating

Source: American College of Sports Medicine

Definitions of the Nutrients You Eat:

WATER:

The most important nutrient is water. You can go without food for several weeks because your body can store it and use it later. But we can't store water. Just a few days without water could cause death. Over half of your body is made up of water. Whenever you cry, sweat, breathe out or go to the bathroom your body loses some water. If you blow on a cold mirror, you can see the water in your breath. You can get water in the fluids you drink, such as milk and juice. Fruits and vegetables also help supply your body with water.

CARBOHYDRATES:

This is your major source of energy. It's important to eat carbohydrates throughout the day, especially before and after your sports practice or games. You get most of your carbohydrates from bread, cereal, fruits and vegetables.

PROTEIN:

This nutrient helps you build muscle and repair body cells. Eating foods high in protein such as low-fat or skim milk, lean meats, low-fat cheese and eggs help you grow tall and strong.

CHOLESTEROL:

We make this in our liver and eat it in some of our foods. It circulates in our blood. Too much cholesterol in our blood may lead to build-up in our arteries, making it difficult for blood to travel around our body. It is recommended that we don't eat more than 300mg of cholesterol each day. Because egg yolks are high in cholesterol, we suggest limiting your egg yolks to only two to three each week.

MINERALS:

These nutrients are important for health. They are part of many cells, including the hard ones like bones, teeth and nails. Some common ones are listed on the next page.

CALCIUM:

This is important to help your bones and teeth grow strong. Calcium-rich foods include low-fat or skim milk, low-fat cheese, yogurt and ice cream.

Definitions of the Nutrients You Eat:

IRON:

Red blood cells contain iron, a mineral that makes it possible for oxygen to be transported to the cells. If you don't get enough iron, your cells can't carry as much oxygen and you feel tired. Iron-rich foods include meat, dried beans, breads and cereals. Eating foods high in vitamin C, such as oranges and strawberries, helps your body absorb the iron in foods even better.

ZINC:

This is important for wound healing, preventing illnesses, protein metabolism and growth. Good sources of zinc include meat, seafood, eggs and milk.

SODIUM:

This mineral is important in maintaining fluid balance, helping nerves function and maintaining muscle activity. But too much sodium may increase blood pressure in some people and can be harmful to someone who has heart failure or kidney failure. It is recommended that we keep our sodium intake to less than 2400 mg each day. To do this, avoid using the salt shaker and eating salty foods.

VITAMINS:

Vitamins do not provide energy, but they do help your body process the energy you get from foods.

VITAMINS A AND C:

These are important for healthy skin, hair and nails. Foods rich in Vitamins A and C include many of your fruits and vegetables such as carrots, oranges, squash, potatoes and strawberries.

B VITAMINS:

These help keep your blood healthy. They also help your body produce energy. They are found in meats and enriched grain products.

FAT-SOLUBLE VITAMINS:

These vitamins are carried through your body by fat. They include Vitamins A, D, E and K and provide a variety of important functions.

Food for thought!

FAT:

This nutrient is another source of energy. There are different kinds of fat. One kind is called "saturated fat" and is found in foods that come from animals such as whole milk, cheese, bologna, hot dogs and fatty hamburgers. This kind of fat is bad for your heart health. However, there are other kinds of fats, called "monounsaturated fats" and "polyunsaturated fats," which are found in vegetable oils and nuts. Including these in your daily diet ensures you get the essential fatty acids your body needs to function properly.

Did you know small amounts of some fats are good for your heart?
Here's how to separate what's better fat — and what's harmful.

CHOOSE MORE OFTEN **UNSATURATED FATS**	**CHOOSE LESS OFTEN** **SATURATED FATS**
Canola and olive oil	Fat on meat, turkey and chicken
Tub margarine The label should say "No trans fats"	Butter
	Whole milk and cheese
Nuts, avocados and seeds	Bologna, hot dogs and lunch meats

Make a Sandwich

You can be as creative as you like in making a sandwich. A sandwich can be more than meat between two pieces of bread. You don't need to use loaf bread at all. Try a pita pocket or bagel. Vegetables can jazz up a sandwich, too.

As far as filling goes, expand your options beyond deli meat.

If you prefer deli meat, many kinds of lean and fat-free cuts are available and many taste as good as the fattier versions. Combine two or three kinds of lean cuts such as turkey, ham or roast beef to make a club sandwich.

Try mixing and matching from this handy list. Pick one ingredient from each list to make your own sandwich. Name your sandwich and share your recipe with friends and family.

LIST A — the outside!

Whole wheat bread
Bagel
Tortilla
Pita bread

LIST B — the inside stuff.

Lean turkey breast
Lean ham
Tuna fish
Peanut butter

LIST C — some veggies to add.

Lettuce leaf
Tomato slices
Green pepper slices
Carrot sticks

LIST D — the condiments.

Mustard
Ketchup
Low-fat mayonnaise
Hot sauce

Yak Fact • • • • • • • • • • • • • • • •

National Sandwich Day, named in honor of the Earl of Sandwich, is November 3. He's the English lord who invented the sandwich. Most stories trace the earl's invention back to a late-night card game more than 200 years ago. The earl was hungry, but he didn't want to end the game. He asked his butler to bring some bread and roast beef to the card table. The rest is history!

Fruits and Vegetables that Pack Power!

All fruits and vegetables are good fruits and vegetables. Not only do they keep us healthy, they taste good, too. And talk about convenient packaging, most of them are ready to eat after just washing them! However, some fruits and vegetables do pack more of a nutritious punch than others. Here are our choices of some powerful fruits and vegetables.

Apricots	Orange
Asparagus	Papaya
Broccoli	Spinach
Cantaloupe	Squash
Carrots	Star fruit (carambola)
Corn	Strawberries
Grapefruit	Sweet bell peppers
Kale	Sweet potatoes
Kiwifruit	Tomatoes
Mango	Watermelon

INDEX

INDEX

INDEX

What is Yak's Corner?

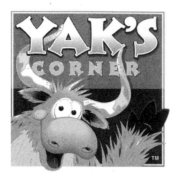

The mission of Yak's Corner — the mini-newspaper for kids produced by the Detroit Free Press — is to empower children with the necessary tools for learning.

Learning to read means connecting to the real world. Kids read best when they see a purpose.

Yak's Corner provides stories that range from hard-hitting news in terms kids can understand to profiles of news-makers and even recipes and crafts.

Yak's Corner explores everything important in the world of young readers. The Yak's Corner program shows children that through reading and understanding, they can make a difference.

Yak's Corner rewards literacy in big ways and small beyond the printed supplements. Year-round, the furry friendly mascot visits schools and libraries.

Young readers are also invited to join the Yak Pack — and become full-fledged members with their family's newspaper subscription to the Detroit Free Press. Members of the club receive a goodie pack including a stuffed baby Yak. Call 800-395-3300 for details.

During summer months, Yak holds a reading club, rewarding summer readers with a party in the fall. The biggest reward is the reading itself — content that is fresh, fun and empowering.

What is Heart Smart®?

Heart Smart® is a health promotion program of the Henry Ford Heart and Vascular Institute. The Heart Smart® program was developed by physicians, physiologists, registered dietitians and community leaders. Through cooperative efforts with organizations, businesses, retail food outlets and corporations, Heart Smart® helps consumers become more aware of how food and lifestyle choices affect their health. Heart Smart® is for informational purposes only, and not for the purpose of giving medical advice, or consultation for any specific condition.

The Henry Ford Heart and Vascular Institute is involved in many projects and activities, all geared toward increasing public awareness about the link between lifestyle and heart health. For more information about the Heart Smart® Program, call 313-972-1920 or go to our Web site at **www.henryford.com.** Heart Smart® is a registered trademark of the Henry Ford Heart and Vascular Institute at 800-HENRY FORD.

The Heart Smart® Kids cookbook is one of three cookbooks published jointly with the Detroit Free Press and Henry Ford Healthy System. Adults: You can order any of these cookbooks by phone. Call 800-245-5082, weekdays from 8 a.m. to 5 p.m. with your VISA or Mastercard.

NOTES

NOTES

NOTES